YOU ARE
GOOD ENOUGH

YOU ARE GOOD ENOUGH

Overcoming Feelings of Inadequacy

Robert J. Furey

A Crossroad Book
The Crossroad Publishing Company
New York

The Crossroad Publishing Company
www.crossroadpublishing.com

Printed in the United States of America

Library of Congress Cataloging-in-Publication Data
Furey, Robert J.
    You are good enough : overcoming feelings of inadequacy / by Robert
J. Furey.
        p.   cm.
    Includes bibliographical references.
    ISBN 0-8245-1957-4 (alk. paper)
    1. Self-esteem – Religious aspects.   I. Title.
BL629.5.S44 F87 2001
152.4 – dc21   2001001310

To my wife, Jane,
and to our children,
Shawn, Colleen, Annie,
Kelly, and Danny

Contents

Introduction

This is a book for people who feel inadequate. More precisely, it is for people whose sense of inadequacy has interfered with their personal growth, happiness, and level of achievement. Everyone knows what it's like to feel inadequate. And, at tolerable levels, inadequacy can even be motivating. Childhood, for instance, is a journey that attempts to turn "can'ts" into "I cans." Our early years acquaint us all with the sense of being too small, too weak, or, simply, too powerless. Fortunately, many people find the encouragement, support, and good fortune to rise above their challenges. They develop the confidence to believe they can be good enough.

Alfred Alder once wrote: "Everyone has a feeling of inferiority. But the feeling of inferiority is not a disease, it is rather a stimulant to healthy, normal striving and development." The doubts we have about ourselves can motivate us to become everything we are meant to be. Or they can grow to the point where they imprison us and keep us miserable and far from our potential.

You Are Good Enough is for those who are handicapped by self-doubts. It's for those who struggle to feel good enough, those whose sense of inferiority is seldom motivating, and, even when it does motivate, it robs them of the feeling of accomplishment. There are, of course, successful people who feel inadequate. But they don't feel successful. They feel phony—as if they don't deserve what they've achieved and their flaws could be revealed at any time.

More often, people who live with significant feelings of inadequacy are underachievers. They don't challenge themselves as much has they could. They don't dream as big as they should. They conclude that risks will lead to failure and thus fear that their disguise will eventually fail them.

If you are ruled by feelings of inadequacy, you are prejudiced against yourself. You are not giving yourself a chance to prove yourself. The judge and jury in your head are unfair. You are convicting yourself without an honest trial. You may need to change your thinking. And, perhaps more than anything, you will need to practice hope.

You Are Good Enough begins with a description of shame. You need to know that you are not the only one who feels this way. Sometimes the first step toward healing is knowing that you are not alone. There are many people who feel badly about themselves. But many people emerge from this darkness with a confidence in themselves and a passion for life. You may not believe this now but, please, read on. For now, I am only asking that you invest a little hope and consider opening a few doors.

Dark mines produce gold. Learn about the darkness. Then reach for the gold.

Chapter One

If People Knew
the Real Me...

You're not like the others. You don't measure up. You're not good enough. You don't know for certain when it began, even though you may have some clues. But for some time now, you've been different. You're not as good as they are. You're not as competent. You don't have what they do. You're not sure how many people know of your inadequacy, but you suspect that quite a few do. Even if they never put it in words, you fear that they know.

At times, you look inside yourself to try to understand how you got this way. This self-examination, though, never really lasts long. You're sure that the unknown parts of you are as flawed as the ones you already know, so what would be the point in looking for more pain? You may have sought help from a counselor, clergyman, family doctor, or psychiatrist. But you didn't tell them everything, did you? No, you left out the worst parts. Then again, maybe you've never gone to anyone for help. Asking for help implies an ability to hope and trust, two qualities you can't seem to hold on to.

It's hard for you to accept that you deserve happiness, justice, friendship, love, or intimacy. You may even feel unworthy of good health. You settle too easily. You don't make enough demands on life because doing so might expose you. This is not tolerated. Your voice, particularly when it communicates

11

who you really are, should not be heard. Your true identity must be kept hidden.

You've become a master at keeping secrets. Although you worry that those around you can easily identify your inadequacies, this is probably not the case. You are very good at hiding. You hide your feelings, hopes, dreams, creative ideas, and hurts. At one time this took a great deal of conscious effort, but now it seems as if hiding comes naturally. At this point it seems that continuing to hide requires less energy than it would to be honest and spontaneous.

Keeping so much of yourself tucked away makes intimacy difficult. Intimacy is about sharing yourself with someone. This requires self-disclosure and self-expression. You won't risk this. Letting others that close would put them in a position to see the flaws. Once they get a look at these, you're sure they will leave you.

There may, indeed, be people whom you love very much. You are capable of loving someone desperately. Furthermore, you feel the need for friendship and may be more than willing to sacrifice for the good of others. This willingness to please others may be so strong that it leads to exhaustion. Through hard work, you attempt to compensate for what you lack. It may never have occurred to you that your inherent goodness is a marvelous gift to share with someone. More likely, you don't feel your goodness at all. But you can offer money, sex, a constant willingness to work someone else's shift, or you can tolerate repeated abuses of one kind or another. You can be used and manipulated all because you believe assertiveness leads to abandonment.

You've always been aware of your need for people. You've tried to convince yourself at times that this wasn't so, but you've never really lost touch with the knowledge that you are a creature that needs people. You live in a bind. You want people near you, but you fear revealing yourself. You feel you can't afford to let others see the real you. You live by one variation or another of the creed: "If people knew the real me, they would leave me." Maybe the particular wording in your head is more like: "If people knew the real me, they wouldn't love me or respect me." Or perhaps: "They would ridicule me." You have lived with this monster for so long that it operates on autopilot and may now live in your unconscious outside of your awareness.

You want people close to you but not close enough to get a good look inside you. You may pull people close to you and then, for reasons they cannot comprehend, push them away. Some people, sad to say, spend their lives this way. Pull and push. Pull and push. Or maybe you've created a buffer zone around you that keeps folks from getting too close. If so, you've become skilled at keeping them at this distance. You live with the hope that, "If people never know the real me, maybe they'll stay."

You walk the line between loneliness and exposure. You may have become adept at this. Still, it never comes easy. Since you have trouble believing that you have gifts in the first place, this is hard for you to understand. You probably miss the fact that you have a powerful personal radar system that can recognize pain in other people. You feel what most other people miss. You can see another person's broken heart or another's feelings of self-loathing even when this suffering is unrecognized by others. This talent for empathy is both a blessing and an affliction. It helps connect you with people (the blessing). It also pulls people to move close to you (the curse). If you can focus on the other person's pain, you feel more comfortable. If that person, though, should get close enough to see your scars, you may become a skunk and do something to push them away.

Your need for other people is, by and large, fueled by your need for their approval. Oh, you may tell yourself that you don't need anyone else's affirmation, but you do. You don't accept yourself. Consequently, without their acceptance, you have nothing. If others don't approve of you, then no one does. This condition can't be tolerated for long. You may have to compromise your values, but you will find someone to acknowledge and applaud something about you. If you have lived through extended periods of time without feeling anyone's approval, you may have even considered self-destruction.

Your feelings of inadequacy may have developed a force of their own. If so, they color your perceptions in ways that empower and maintain your doubts about yourself. You are a criticism magnet. If there is an insult out there for you— no matter how small—you will seize it and attach yourself to it. You don't understand this, but it feels so natural. You will swim through a sea of compliments to reach and swallow a negative evaluation of yourself. You don't like it and may, on the outside, attack it forcefully, but, all and all, it seems appropriate. You may, indeed, provoke the one who criticizes you as a way of generating more criticism for yourself.

Your days are remembered by all the evidence you've collected on how inferior you are. Should you receive many compliments and a single criticism on a given day, at night, when your head hits the pillow, it is that criticism that plants its flag on the top of your psyche. And if you experience a period of time when you are not adequately denigrated, you may alter reality to get your needed dose of castigation. You will turn neutral statements into rebukes. A boss, for instance, who asks the harmless question, "How are you today?" will be interpreted as questioning your work ethic or implying that something appears wrong with you.

Your feelings of inferiority color your memories. You lock on to the painful ones—the embarrassments, failures, and humiliations. You see what you believe. You believe you are defective, and you interpret your experiences accordingly. The price you pay is that you accumulate memories that serve as evidence of your inadequacy.

In spite of the discomfort that you know all too well, you feel an urge to be connected with and approved by others. You want people near you but don't want them to see the real you. So you compromise. You build a false self, a facade that hides the real you. You invest an enormous amount of time and effort tending to this outer self. You never feel that it's perfect (because you are incapable of doing anything that well), but it is vastly superior to the real you. Through your false self, you live the role of something you are not. In this role you may be confident, social, and self-assured. You may present yourself with lots of self-esteem and a never-say-die attitude that indicates inner courage and conviction. Your persona may be so impressive that it causes others to envy you.

Having a good false self keeps people attracted to you and also keeps them from looking inside you where all the bad stuff lives. Unfortunately, for many people the closest they get to real intimacy is to have others fall in love with the role they play. Having someone care for you for the wrong reason, though, is preferable to loneliness. Recognition and appreciation of the mask you wear helps, but it does little to heal the inadequacy you feel. Furthermore, you live with the fear that the mask will slip and you will be exposed.

Because you hide your true self, you fear anything that might bring the real you into the light of day. Consequently, emotions are quite threatening. Although others may describe you, at times, as being emotional, this isn't quite true. You hold back emotionally. Or, more accurately, you hold back as long as you possibly can. Then, when you can no longer keep your feelings contained, they burst to the surface. But even then there's a twist. If you have to show a feeling, you prefer it to be an emotion that keeps people away. You try to turn all your emotions into a single emotion—anger. This anger can be severe. And even though you know better than most how it hurts to be shamed, too often your anger is expressed in a way that shames others.

Expressing honest feeling is too much self-disclosure for you. If you allow yourself to show softer feelings such as sorrow, you feel bad about it later. Maybe you cried in front of a friend and then felt bad because you did. Many people who feel inadequate are ashamed of their feelings. Of all your emotions, you may be particularly ashamed of your fear and hurt.

If you've kept your feelings hidden away for too long, you may present yourself more like a robot than the warm human being you really are. You will always be sensitive, and this is a gift. You can be hurt, and this is a gift, too. You are capable of feeling your own pain and—though you may not show it— you are able to feel the pain that others carry. One of the biggest injustices of your life is that others don't get to see your inner beauty. And because you are so convinced that you are unlovable, neither do you. You don't see your own inner beauty.

No, rather, you are plagued with petty jealousies. You envy those who remind you of what you lack. You may not admit to it, but it's there. In an attempt to salvage some degree of self-respect, you try to attach yourself to people, groups, or teams that receive appreciation. You may be a sports fanatic, or you may remind everyone you know that your sister is a brain surgeon or that your brother is president of the school board. This is self-esteem by association. You have difficulty feeling good about who you are so you try to gain respect through what you root for and whom you know.

You may brag to others about the successes of your siblings or your childhood friends, but deep inside you can't escape the envy. Their competence reminds you of your incompetence. You don't measure up. You may not remember the last time you really made the grade. You measure yourself against standards that always seem beyond your grasp. There are miles between the person you feel you need to be and the person you feel you are; that idealized self may have been created by your parents, your spouse, or society. Somehow, you've received the message that you have to be a such-and-such in order to be acceptable. Usually, this such-and-such is someone else's ideal that you've taken as your own. You've internalized the belief, "If I'm not a such-and-such, I'm a nobody." You've lost track of the fact that not everyone is meant to be a such-and-such. You may have been meant to be a something else.

Your shame has taken a great deal of happiness and health out of your life. At some level you realize this. You would like to change, but any real attempt at change would make you vulnerable to failure, and you're not sure if you could survive another defeat. It probably hasn't sunk in how much you've survived or how much pain you've carried. You don't give yourself credit for such feats. Your victories, if you've noticed them at all, don't mean much to you.

Some might think that you would find peace in sleep, but this isn't the case. You tend to ruminate while trying to get to sleep. Typically, you dwell on something you think you've done wrong, or a remark that you perceive to have been an insult will keep running through your head. Then, once you get to sleep, you're more likely to have unpleasant dreams. If you remember your dreams, you will probably recognize some of the classics. You arrive at work or school only to realize you're still in your underwear or pajamas, or someone is chasing you and you can't run away fast enough, or you are being attacked and you can't defend yourself. Your dreams have themes of inadequacy. You can't do what is expected of you. You are exposed as inferior. These inadequacy dreams can take many forms, but they are usually about being unable to do what needs to be done. A middle-aged man with significant feelings of inferiority told me of one of his dreams where he saw himself playing left field in a baseball game before a large crowd. Each time the ball was hit to him, however, he lacked the strength to throw the ball back into the infield. This man had a long history of humiliation dreams.

If your shame has been severe enough, you may have thought about suicide. Your strength (something you don't give yourself enough credit for) has kept you alive through the most difficult times. You may also fear what would happen to you if you killed yourself. Good things don't happen to bad people like you, so it's hard for you to believe that anything positive is waiting for you if you end your life. Also, you've never been able to completely understand it, but there has always been a force inside you pushing to keep you alive.

As long as your self-dislike continues, your spiritual dimension will never be what it could be. You will probably drift through a variety of religious attitudes as the years pass. Even if you believe in God, you will not honestly reveal yourself to him. Again, one of your greatest fears is honest self-revelation. You may try to convince yourself that you've revealed all there is to reveal, but deep inside you know this isn't the case.

Your spiritual and emotional lives are stunted for the same reason. One of the most powerful forces (if not *the* most powerful force) in your life is a lie. You are shaped by that lie. The lie pervades you and impacts all who come near you. You don't really have a personality; you have a lie. This lie makes you miserable and drains the life from you, but you hold it sacred all the same. The lie is conducting a reign of terror inside you. You dare not challenge it for fear that your secrets will be revealed. The lie and the secrets. They have far too much control in your life.

The lie tells you that you will never be good enough. It's not so much that you've *done* something wrong. Rather, the lie tells you that you *are* something wrong. You are weak, dirty, and defective. You don't have what it takes, and you may never have what you need to be adequate. Perhaps there was a time when you were worthy of respect, but those days are gone. You're damaged goods now. The lie tells you that no one really wants to help you and, even if they did, there's not much anyone can do to improve you anyway. The lie insists your shame is well deserved. The lie says you're simply not good enough.

Maybe you make feeble attempts to challenge the lie, but you stop short of making a full-scale assault on this tyrant. You know how the lie punishes when it's challenged. It incites all those memories that support it and marches them into your consciousness. It raises the memories of all those slights, failures, defeats, insults, and humiliations that have led you to believe you are inadequate. These all lead you to follow the lie. For instance, on a good day, you may feel strong enough to reinvent yourself. Maybe you've listened to an inspirational speech or read a book that has convinced you that you don't have to feel inferior. You start to gain confidence in yourself. But then the lie calls all those hard memories to mind. A crack begins to grow in your confidence. Just enough of a crack to introduce doubt. Just enough doubt to sabotage your success. Just enough sabotage to revive those feelings of inferiority.

You're not good enough because you believe the lie that says you're not good enough. The longer you live the lie, the truer it becomes. As this condition continues, it can grow deeper and more powerful.

The lie is an abusive master. It constantly points to your inadequacies—real or imagined. You tend to begin new ventures with an attitude that says, "I can't do it." Your shame keeps you from emerging as your real beautiful self. As long as you live this lie, you will never be fully born. You will never emerge as the wonderful human being you are meant to be.

Shame is a lie, but, in strange way, it protects you. If you never show the real you, it's less likely that you will be hurt. If you keep your real self hidden away, you feel safer, less vulnerable. This protection factor has kept you from doing all you can to conquer your feelings of inferiority. Your inferiority, with all its costs, offers some security. And it's quite easy to prove your inadequacy. If at any point the lie seems to be slipping away, you can—consciously or unconsciously—do something else to demonstrate that you are not quite good enough.

You have doubts about whether your situation will ever improve. Besides, if others knew the real you, they wouldn't have much hope for you either (would they?).

I'd like to offer you some hope at this point, but it probably wouldn't help. Not yet. You may be unwilling to change because you are tired of being disappointed. Or perhaps you're used to running behind "experts" who offer painless miracle cures. This hasn't helped much, right? More likely, you have little hope for recovery. Thus, anyone who offers you hope will be disqualified as a fraud. This would just be another case of people offering something they couldn't possibly deliver.

Please understand that there is hope. But before we get there, you must understand more about the lie.

"Inferiority," "shame," "inadequacy," and "defectiveness" are all words used to describe this condition. Any of them will do. People who live with the feeling that they are simply not good enough have many more ways of articulating this dreaded condition. They may say, "I'm weak," "I'm awful," "I'll never be what I should be," "I'm a loser," or "I'll never be loved." Some people afflicted with shame have a favorite description they use to abuse themselves. Others use a never-ending series of caustic remarks to degrade themselves.

The fundamental dimension of inferiority is the belief that one is significantly less than one needs to be. For example, an adult male patient of mine who had lived most of his life with deep-seated shame once told me that he had always fallen short of "the standards." When I asked him, "Which standards?" he replied, "Pick a standard. Any standard." He wasn't a failure because of something specific he had done. He was inadequate because of who he was. He felt himself to be wrong all over.

This distinction is important. We are not talking about guilt here. Guilt is the feeling that "I've *done* something wrong." Shame, on the other hand, laments the fact that "I *am* something wrong." Shame runs deeper than guilt. It gets rooted much further into our beings. If you believe your behavior is inappropriate, you will feel guilt. If, however, you feel you are not the person you need to be, you will feel shame.

People find it much easier to talk about guilt. Indeed, we live in an age where confessing one's transgression, whether that be in therapy or on a talk show, has become more routine than ever. But shame will never be in style. It is too painful. Acknowledging mistakes is one thing. Exposing oneself as inadequate is quite another.

People who are filled with shame sometimes try to convince themselves that they are really only dealing with guilt. Not long ago, for instance, a middle-aged woman told me, "No, I don't feel shame. I just feel guilty about everything!" What became clear was that she was filled with shame. At first, she didn't want to admit it to herself or to me. It took her some time to realize that the reason she made so many wrong choices was that she believed she was incapable of making healthy choices. And when she made a good choice, she was still so down on herself that she convinced herself that she had once again made a bad move. She wouldn't let herself recognize and accept a victory because she had become sure that she was nothing but a loser.

None of us wants to find feelings of inferiority within ourselves. Few experiences hurt more than being left out. Guilt is a more tolerable feeling than shame. Yet shame may be the more common. It is certainly the more damaging. Shakespeare understood the importance of shame to the human condition. He wrote about shame about nine times more often than guilt.[1] He saw humanity's hidden epidemic.

In his book *The Culture of Shame,* psychiatrist Andrew P. Morrison defines shame as

> a feeling of self-castigation which arises when we are convinced that there is something about ourselves that is wrong, inferior, flawed, weak, or dirty. Shame is fundamentally a feeling of loathing against ourselves, a hateful vision of ourselves through our own eyes—although this vision may be determined by how we expect or believe other people are experiencing us. Generally speaking, this self-vision is accompanied by self-consciousness, and by a conviction of important failure that often generates a wish to hide or conceal.[2]

Those who feel inadequate keep an eye on themselves, trying to keep their defectiveness hidden. The goal of shame is to hide. In the more severe cases, the aim is to disappear completely.

Feeling inferior is more than a symptom. It is, as psychiatrist Donald L. Nathanson writes, a shaper of symptoms.[3] It can produce any of a number of symptoms. Inferiority can lead to depression, anxiety, addiction, self-destructiveness, hostility, shyness, academic difficulties, underachievement, fear of change, eating disorders, and loneliness. Certain authorities on the subject have even discussed a disorder sometimes called "shame psychosis." In this state, people become so overwhelmed by feelings of self-loathing that they may lose touch with reality.

Shame can spread through one's being. Psychologist Gershen Kaufman refers to it as a malignant cancer. It is, he says, "an inner torment."[4] It is, perhaps, the most disturbing of all feelings. Once shame takes root, it begins to bias all our perceptions. Those afflicted then look at life through a distorted lens. Compliments are not accepted because they are not believed. Criticisms, though, are given great credibility. Inferiority is a self-fulfilling prophecy. It molds reality to fit its expectations.

As the sickness grows, it takes on a voice, a voice capable of whispering, or screaming, demeaning words like, "You're not wanted," or, "You'll never be good enough." Sometimes people know the source of this torment. They may recognize these as the words of their parent, stepparent, or teacher. Other people cannot identify the source of their ridicule. They only know these voices never leave for long.

No one accepts inferiority without a fight. It's simply too painful for us to welcome it into our lives. Small children who are verbally degraded by their caretakers, for instance, will not readily accept what they are hearing. Instead, they will use whatever mechanisms are available to them to escape the onslaught. A three-year-old may try desperately to be a perfect child (i.e., everything the parent wants her to be) in order to stop the shaming. A four-year-old may call upon superhero strength to build a superhero self-image to protect himself. He may empower himself with defiance and tantrums. A five-year-old may attempt to survive her parents' neglect by building a rich fantasy world that provides for her need to be loved.

These defenses are seldom adequate, and when the defenses are defeated, so is the child. Shame usually begins with the conclusion, "I'm not as good as I need to be." In spite of whatever gifts and talents may emerge, this developing child continues to believe, "I'm not as good as I need to be."

Consider Alex, a fifty-three-year-old man who worked most of his life as a teacher. By the time he came to see me, he had been in a wide variety of psychological and psychiatric treatment programs. Over the years, he had presented a number of different symptoms and had been diagnosed with over a dozen psychiatric disorders. The one constant was Alex's feelings of inadequacy. He told me on several occasions that "the only thing that I'm good at is being a psychiatric patient." This, of course, was not at all true. Alex was a good man who cared deeply for people. Most of the time, he had a marvelous sense of humor that fueled an infectious laugh. He was highly sensitive and could empathize well with people in pain. This sensitivity, however, made him emotionally vulnerable to the bumps and bruises that come with everyday living.

Alex had a wonderful gift for music, but he insisted that it was nothing special. "Anyone can play as well as I can," he used to say. "They just have to practice." Seemingly without the ability to affirm himself, Alex went through life collecting hurts, and those hurts began showing up at an early age. His father was a mean alcoholic who verbally abused his family on a regular basis. His mother, although heroic in her attempts to protect her children, could offer little help. She had her own deep feelings of inadequacy and thus lacked the personal power to improve her context. Growing up, Alex was hit by a double whammy. His father debased him, and his mother carried a shaming voice inside herself that chanted, "You're so awful, of course, your children will be problems."

Alex grew up damaged. In spite of the gifts others could see in him, he could only see his wounds. The injuries inflicted upon him caused a sort of blindness. He could not see his beauty. Because he could not see his blessings, he doubted, and even disqualified, those who pointed to their existence. He could only see the darkness. So there he lived, surrounded by his flaws—the real ones and the imagined ones as well.

Then there are others, like Susan, who develop feelings of inadequacy later in life. Susan was one of six children and was considered the brightest and most beautiful of the litter. She recognized early how people valued her looks and her intelligence, and she felt secure that she would always be appreciated. During her teenage years, however, her life began to change. Her moods became erratic. She knew her family had a history of mental illness, but she assumed she would be immune to this. As her condition deteriorated, her parents started taking her to what became a long series of doctors. At first, they used generic terms such as "mood disorder" and "depressive disorder." Then, in time, the diagnostic picture cleared—bipolar disorder. She was living on a roller coaster, with her emotions taking her down to the depths of depression and then climbing to manic periods where she felt the strength of the gods. In between these extremes, she lived for extended intervals in a stable zone where everything appeared fine.

As serious as bipolar disorder can be, Susan faced a bigger obstacle. The diagnosis forced her to change how she looked at herself. No longer the perfect child whom everyone seemed to adore, she was now damaged in a way that threatened her place in the universe. She once felt she belonged almost everywhere. Now, she questioned if she would be wanted anywhere.

Susan refused to accept the diagnosis. She denied the problems, which escalated as time passed. To have this illness meant she would be inadequate, inferior, and alone. She knew there were treatments for her illness but, to Susan, this was a moot point. Since she denied her condition, she had no cause to consider treatment.

As her illness worsened, her denial became more of a full-time job. She blamed others for her misfortunes. She began to hide by distancing herself from her family and those who knew her best, contacting them only during her ever decreasing periods of self-confidence. She continued to date, but her tastes in men reflected her growing shame. She gave up on being loved so she focused on being needed. Toward this end, she availed herself of a very needy man. During what may have been a manic episode, she ended this relationship, soon found another man just as needy, and married shortly thereafter.

Now in her late thirties, Susan dances on the fringes of help. She has had several encounters with short-term counseling and "new age" healing experiences. She rarely asks for help for herself; instead she spends her "healing" time trying to understand why others disappoint her.

Alex and Susan feel worse than inadequate. They feel unlovable. Alex can't remember feeling loved, but he vaguely remembers his mother trying to love him. Susan remembers the feeling of being loved. She plays these memories over and over in her head. She grieves the loss of that love. As time passes, she becomes more and more convinced that such love will never come again. They are both living scripts of inferiority. Alex acquired his role early in life. Susan took the part later on. They each know how inferior people should live, and, in their own ways, they try to make the best of being failures.

In both these people, it is rather clear when and how their shame started. With others, it is not so obvious. Many people live plagued with serious doubts about themselves and never really understand why. Everyone carries shaming memories. Everyone who has ever had a childhood knows what it's like to feel small and powerless. But most people grow beyond these experiences. They use powerlessness as incentive to grow more powerful. But far too many souls get caught in powerlessness. They lack the confidence to rise above it. In short, they simply feel they can't.

Feelings of inferiority are easier to understand when they are rooted in identifiable circumstances such as abuse, neglect, or chronic illness. Although these tragedies do not kill the confidence of everyone who experiences them, they do provide the type of assault that would understandably injure a human being's self-image. Those whose inadequacy begins in these arenas have a place to point to and, perhaps, begin healing. They are aware of what they may be trying to hide.

Many others lack this awareness. Shame is carried in scenes or memories, but these experiences can be hidden so deeply that they are unknown to those who carry them. Shame is learned. Some folks, however, have forgotten how they learned it. These unfortunate individuals are tormented by ghosts that lack form, substance, and a clear story. Still, they haunt their victims with a chilling message that says they will never be good enough to belong anywhere.

A person who cannot answer the question, "Why do I feel so bad about myself?" can always create an answer. She can make the kinds of decisions that will cause her to feel defective. She may act out sexually or aggressively, compromise any or all of her values, hurt a friend or loved one, or ignore all that she cares for. She may then explain her self-loathing with shallow conclusions such as, "I'm always screwing things up," or, "I always end up hurting the people I love." She says this in a way that implies she cannot help herself, that her failures are merely the result of her *being* a failure. In reality, she is deliberately (although perhaps unconsciously) creating events that will help explain the ghosts inside her that insist she is unlovable. This behavior will not lead to healing. It will, however, give this person a reason for feeling the way she does.

While these shaming activities add to one's feelings of inadequacy, they do nothing to help one find the causes or the cure. All of us can, at almost any time, prove our inadequacy. With each self-defeating decision we make, the deeper we fall into shame. Self-defeating behaviors can prove our inadequacy, but they will not enlighten or reveal how the feelings of inferiority began. Shame often begins in childhood, but it can start at any point in a person's life. In all cases, however, shame begins when our true self comes under attack—overtly or covertly, subtly or blatantly—with such force that we can no longer defend ourselves. As a result of this assault, the wounded yet true self is hidden away to avoid continued damage. It is placed out of reach of all who might hurt it. It then gets watched as carefully as one would watch a fragile infant. We take extreme care that this true self does not appear, for fear that it will be criticized, ridiculed, or humiliated. The best defense is to hide the injured self.

Shame is a form of protection. It is an attitude—a lie— that insists people hide who they really are. They must hide for fear that they will be evaluated negatively. Hiding prevents the inevitable humiliation. Shame is an attitude and a feeling. It is the attitude that says, "Don't show your real face." It is also that awful feeling that comes when one is, or is about to be, exposed as inadequate.

Shame fights its antidote. When someone who has lived with shame tries to build confidence, the voice of shame calls attention to all the risks involved. Shame points to every possible landmine that could explode in your face. It exaggerates the risks to the point of absurdity. A man in his late forties, for instance, in the midst of trying to recover from a lifetime of feeling inferior, once said to me, "I honestly believed that if people saw the real me that I *would die.*"

Interestingly, this man's inadequacy tried to become a self-fulfilling prophecy. Whenever he would move toward a confident, honest expression of himself, he experienced discomfort, sometimes extreme discomfort. On numerous occasions, he had what are sometimes called shame attacks. During such attacks, shame fills a person with the power of a tidal wave. It owns a person and communicates in every possible way how loathsome he is. It is simply too powerful to deny or avoid. These episodes can last for hours, a duration that can seem like an eternity. On rare occasions, they can even last for days. Typically, the pain begins to subside as soon as the person promises to go back into hiding. Once this occurs, shame has little reason to waste any more of its energy.

Someone who feels inadequate does not want to be who she is. She wants to be stronger and more desirable. She wants to be respectable and worthy of appreciation. Inferiority feelings tell her she is simply not enough. Not good enough, worthy enough, acceptable enough. Just not enough. Shame leads her to believe she does not have what it takes to be good enough. Feeling inferior, for many, becomes a life sentence.

As this condition deteriorates, shame becomes so uncomfortable that it can no longer be tolerated. Here there are two choices: work through it or repress it. Working through it is the healthy option, but, as we have discussed, shame does not leave easily. Shame weakens one's confidence, and, without confidence, personal growth is all the more difficult. The other option is to deny the shame. Human beings have an enormous capacity to deny that which pains us. Repressed shame, though, creates its own problems. One of the most common complications is unhealthy anger. The threat of degradation sends one into a defensive mode. In this position, anger seems a logical response. Although the first reaction is to hide, often the next move is to retaliate.

This anger may be expressed in a variety of ways, many of which are quite unhealthy. People dealing with unacknowledged shame may fly into rages. Rage gives them a feeling of power and control, qualities they lack in their everyday lives. This rage may occur routinely, or there may be long stretches between outbursts. Besides the feel of power, rage has a second benefit. It pushes people away. Like the skunk's odor, rage keeps others from getting too close. This distancing technique prevents intimacy and the possibility that our inner self might be exposed. Rage helps keep people lonely. It forces a distance between people. In the short run, it protects those who feel they are too weak to deserve respect.

But in the long run, it only makes matters worse. Those who rage typically feel more ashamed of themselves after they explode. They feel little pride in using tantrums to deal with reality. The outbursts become more evidence of their defectiveness.

Unidentified feelings of inferiority can produce other pathological forms of anger such as passive-aggressiveness. Passive-aggressive people are angry, but they don't feel entitled to their anger. They disguise it in ways that confuse those who bear the brunt of their animosity. A passive-aggressive individual will promise to give you a ride to the doctor's office and then show up late with countless excuses. This person may never raise his voice but he tends to be late when you need him and "forgets" to come through after he promises to. At first, his apologies may seem sincere. In time, though, the pattern becomes clear. His lateness and forgetfulness is his attempt to get even for all the wrongs he believes have been inflicted upon him.

Passive-aggressiveness and rage are two problematic types of anger that focus on other people. But those who believe they are not good enough are also prone to point their hostility in another direction. They sometimes aim all their venom at themselves. They feel deserving of their own wrath. Their self-criticism can be brutal and relentless. So relentless, that after a time it may feel like their normal state. Degrading themselves becomes a steady part of their lives. It feels out of their control and never seems to stop. At this point, they more or less stop fighting back. They merely accept their inner persecutor as something they deserve and must learn to accept. Some people live their lives this way. In other cases, though, people find the courage to challenge the lie.

Not long ago I gave a talk on people who feel bad about themselves. In the back of the room sat a man who appeared to be in his early thirties. As I spoke, I noticed his intense gaze. He remained silent until we were almost finished, and then he raised his hand and told this story with tears in his eyes and in his voice.

"When I was a kid, my stepfather... every night at dinner, he would call me a 'fucking idiot.' Every night. I still hear it. Every day."

His sadness then took his voice away. I won't know how this story ends. I'll probably never know what becomes of him. But there is cause for hope. Although he lived with a great deal of hurt for a long time, he gave some important signs that he may be working through his ordeal. First, he recognized that he needed to let go of his stepfather. His shame will ease when he frees himself from the person who shames him. He has been carrying this person inside him for years. In order to let go of the same, he must let go of the shamer. Second, the fact that he made this disclosure in front of fellow human beings might suggest that he is through hiding his shame and thus began to free his true self. Self-disclosure is one of the first and most important steps toward removing feelings of inadequacy.

When shame is addressed directly, unhealthy expressions of anger decrease. Once the anger gives way, hurt and fear take center stage. Dealing with these two feelings is a difficult yet essential dimension of healing. Both increase our feeling of vulnerability and neither provide the power that anger does. Still, the fear and hurt are real and must be allowed expression.

Those raised in families that discouraged the expression of emotion will have a particularly difficult time with this. It's a sad fact that many children are criticized for showing their feelings. Too often, well-intentioned parents communicate, directly or indirectly, that emotions are a sign of weakness. Their children are left to conclude: "Because I feel, I am weak." They learn to hide their feelings and, in the process, learn to conceal themselves. Sometimes I think this is the single most common experience among the people I have treated over the years. They have spent too much time in contexts that have not allowed them to be who they are. As a result, they have come to believe that who they really are is not good enough.

Sometimes the healthiest looking families are the worst offenders. In their efforts to appear flawless, they refuse to allow for the expression of anything that might tarnish that image.

Human frailties like fear, doubt, hurt, confusion, and failure get hidden, as if being human would disgrace the family. These families enforce the mask of perfection through conditional love. They live by the code: "I will love you only if...."

The best way to prevent feelings of inadequacy is through unconditional love. This is a love that says, "I love you as you are and I love you for the person you are becoming." A child raised with conditional love is much more likely to feel inadequate. A child raised with unconditional love, however, will develop a much healthier psychological immune system. It is much less likely that she will seriously doubt her worth as a person. She will know she is lovable because she has been loved unconditionally.

In many families, the conditional nature of their love is so camouflaged that the growing child never really understands what is going on. Something feels wrong but she can't figure out exactly what that is. In these families, parents may also be unaware of the demands and the disapproval they place on their children. In many dysfunctional families, these parents may be asking their children to compensate for their own feelings of inadequacy. Consciously or unconsciously they ask their children to "be what I can never be" or "be something that makes me appear competent." When the child cooperates with this, she receives approval. When she does not, the approval is withheld.

There are common paths to shame. Even so, all who get there do so in their own way. For some it is fairly easy to understand how they came to doubt their worth. For others it is not as clear how the wounds developed. These people need to examine the events of their lives that have left them feeling defective. This understanding is a part of forgiveness. To be freed from the grasp of inadequacy, people may need to forgive themselves for all the self-inflicted harm. Forgiveness may also be necessary to make peace with those who have hurt them. This sometimes involves reliving painful experiences. At times, a wound must be opened before it can be closed.

Sadly, many people never move beyond their feelings of worthlessness. They spend their lives with the awful effects of self-condemnation. The consequences are many and each person lives with them in a unique way. Everyone who has lived with this condition has something new to teach. Everyone's story is valuable. These stories, we shall see, need to be told.

There are themes in the stories of those who have come to see themselves as less than worthwhile. In these themes we learn the cost of shame. Beside the anger, there are other kinds of pain. Feeling inadequate is a very uncomfortable state. Even those who use alcohol, drugs, sex, work, or any other addiction to distract themselves do not escape the pain, and what help they get from these compulsions eventually disappears. Feelings of inferiority are never cured by addictive behaviors.

Shame keeps one focused on oneself. Those who feel damaged are locked into self-consciousness. They feel surrounded by mirrors, all of which make them look bad. This pain and self-consciousness make it hard to focus for extended periods of time. There is too much grumbling going on inside, and a great deal of energy must be spent keeping all those terrible secrets hidden away. In his book *Shame: The Exposed Self,* psychologist Michael Lewis writes: "Shame disrupts ongoing activity as the self focuses completely on itself, and the result is confusion: inability to think clearly, inability to talk, and inability to act."[5] This inability to think clearly leads to a chronic underachievement that, in turn, produces stronger feelings of inadequacy. This underachievement exists even in those who are still fighting to compensate for their perceived deficiencies. None of us live up to our potential while trying to hide our true selves.

The expression of our true selves is essential if we are to know where we belong. A false self never knows what it feels like to belong. The places where we belong are the places where we can love and be loved. These are the places where we find a purpose to our lives and our work feels productive and meaningful. Many people, of course, believe no such place exists. They can't imagine themselves finding this much happiness. Unfortunately, as long as they think this way, healthy living may not be possible. Until we feel worthy of love and happiness, we will never know what it feels like to really belong.

The loss of belonging is one of the most tragic consequences of inferiority. When faced with a great deal of stress, shamed individuals often convey the thought, "I just want to run away." When asked where they might like to go, they typically respond with a vague nameless destination like, "Anywhere! Just anywhere. Anywhere except here!" This is the cry of those who are looking for a place to belong. They feel a void but don't know where to go or what to do to fill it. Furthermore, they tend not to look for the right place until a crisis hits.

People who just aren't good enough let life pass them by. Sooner or later they tend to fall into passive postures where, at best, they react to the challenges life throws at them. They don't initiate progress and change because they feel too ineffective to get positive results and, besides, such activity might reveal too much of themselves. This self-revelation runs completely contrary to the self-imposed rules they live by. They don't emerge, contribute, and build. They are more likely to hide, daydream, and wait.

Waiting leads to boredom, another common consequence of inferiority. When feelings are repressed, boredom sets in. People who are constantly lamenting, "I don't know what I want to do," might as well be saying, "I don't know how I really feel." In order to enjoy life, we must identify those aspects of life we find enjoyable. This requires a willingness (a) to be in touch with our true selves, and (b) to act on what we discover. In other words, in order to be healthy, happy, and fully alive, we need to identify our needs and be willing to work to meet these needs in a way that is not destructive to others even if this means revealing ourselves to the world. People who feel incomplete repress their desire to take piano lessons or art lessons or learn how to scuba dive. To stay aware of these desires and act upon them would make them feel too childish. They may want to write a book, but this would make them appear conceited and would only result in failure anyway. They daydream about relationships with people they admire, but any movement in this direction would, they are convinced, surely lead to rejection and embarrassment. They prefer safety . . . as life passes by.

Another unfortunate result of shame is envy. Those who feel inferior see the world as filled with people who are superior. They are prone to envy their neighbors, co-workers, college roommates, and family members. Anyone who has something "more" than they do reminds them of their inadequacy. These reminders sting and serve to isolate them from those they envy. And then there's the opposite side of the same coin. Because human beings can only tolerate so much shame, those who constantly compare themselves to others must find at least a few favorable comparisons. They need someone to be worse off than they are. This is the basis for many forms of prejudice, and those judged as being more flawed than they are must be so horrible that they are a proper focus for all of a shamed person's displaced anger. This is one way that shame gets passed on.

Of all the consequences of shame, this is one of the most

hurtful and one that people come to regret deeply when they start to heal. People who feel inadequate want more than anything to be loved by and connected with other human beings. They don't want to distance themselves by judging others. They, of all people, know the pain of shaming and would like, more than anything, to remove this practice from the planet. But their own feelings of inferiority simply bring out the worst in them. They push them to act in ways that make them feel even more ashamed. The shamed too often become shamers. Thus the cancer grows.

The growth of the tumor that is shame can be as destructive as any cancer. In 1931 the eminent psychiatrist Alfred Adler wrote, "No human being can bear a feeling of inferiority for long; he will be thrown into a tension which necessitates some kind of action."[6] People who feel this way will deny, repress, distract, hide, lie, and distort, all to avoid revealing and dealing with what they feel to be true. Some people spend their lives using these defenses and thus drastically reduce what they could do with those lives. Others, either because they refuse to use these defenses or because their defenses cannot control the anguish, face an awareness of their suffering that is so intense it may lead them to consider suicide. Self-loathing and hopelessness are often a lethal combination. We lose far too many beautiful people who end their lives without ever seeing their beauty.

Shame exists on many levels from mild to severe, with each level contributing to some degree of self-destructiveness. At a mild degree inferiority sabotages our relationships, our careers, and our happiness. Severe cases threaten lives. Mild shame can be like a mild infectious disease, which can, left unattended, become fatal.

If you suffer from the condition I am describing, you may not be willing, at least at this point, to hope. Hope is the

beginning of a frightening risk. Hope can lead to disappoint-
ments, and you may have already experienced your share of
these. So, for now, we will continue to try to understand this
condition. We will look at it as it exists at different levels—
mild, moderate, and severe. To understand is to begin to
forgive and heal.

Once you come to understand, perhaps you will be ready
to move on.

Chapter Two

Degrees of Shame

We have all felt inadequate at times. We may not want to remember these occasions, but they are there: moments when we were exposed as not being enough of what someone thought we should be, periods when we fell short of what we believed we ought to be. It's hard to imagine a childhood that does not have its share of difficult memories—memories of failing, striking out, or not having the confidence even to try.

It's not really the memories that cause you to feel inadequate. It's what you do with them. If these memories come to define you, you will feel shame. If, however, you use these scenes to motivate you, you grow. Adler described this situation well:

> Everyone has a feeling of inferiority. But the feeling of inferiority is not a disease, it is rather a stimulant to healthy, normal striving and development. It becomes a pathological condition only when the sense of inadequacy overwhelms the individual and, far from stimulating him to useful activity, makes him depressed and incapable of development.[7]

Inferiority sets in when you feel you cannot improve yourself. Or, more precisely, you feel you cannot improve yourself enough to make yourself respectable, acceptable, lovable, etc.

When who you are is unacceptable and you feel unable

to alter this situation, you feel shame. Shame runs on a continuum from mild to severe. Left unattended, mild feelings
of inadequacy can grow more serious. Some people experience symptoms of mild and moderate shame at the same time.
Others who suffer from this condition cannot recall the mild
symptoms at all. They look at their lives and see only days
filled with crippling shame.

Mild Shame

You don't deserve to feel the way you do. No one does. First of
all, you have more loneliness in your life than a person should.
Sure, there are people around you, but somehow they're not
close enough. There are dimensions of you that you have decided to keep to yourself. At times you've convinced yourself
that you have been completely open and honest with those
who try to get close to you. But in your heart of hearts, you
know you are holding back.

You can be a true friend, one who is willing to sacrifice
for others and would love to be loved. Still, you are cautious
about who you will let near you. You prefer people who won't
look too deep. If they were able to do so, they might leave.
So there is always a distance. Few people see your hurt. On
those occasions when your hurt becomes visible, it will likely
be misunderstood, probably because you point your perceptive
friends in the wrong direction. As painful as loneliness can
be, you prefer loneliness to the threat of anyone seeing how
deficient you are.

You have moments of intimacy, and you are sincerely grateful for them. But they are only moments. You may live for
these moments. But, still, they are only moments. If you were
to heal, you would have more of these moments. Until that
time, these all too brief experiences will have to sustain you.

Chances are, you are a very good worker. The praise of an employer or a co-worker means a lot to you. In the wrong environment, of course, this desire to please others could be exploited. You might be willing to exhaust yourself for the occasional pat on the back. In a healthier environment, though, where your efforts are genuinely appreciated, you could do quite well, especially if you felt valued for the person you are and not just for the products or services you provide.

But here again there is a catch. Due to your feelings of inadequacy, you are skeptical of compliments that come your way. You tend to devalue or disqualify them. They don't feel right. Maybe they're well intended, but it's hard to believe they could be true. It's the criticisms that seem most accurate and so much more believable. You give the criticisms you receive a great deal of power. Add to this the fact that you criticize yourself too harshly and you can see how your confidence takes a pounding.

You have a fear of being ridiculed, and this limits you. Public speaking, for example, may make you quite uncomfortable. To your credit, however, you sometimes face this fear and face it well. But this doesn't lift your confidence much. Just because you weren't humiliated the last hundred times you made a presentation doesn't mean much to you. You are more than aware that your next experience could be a disaster. This fear of the future may not always stop you, but it does take a certain amount of joy out of your life. You don't look forward with as much enthusiasm as others seem to.

You're competitive, possibly too competitive. This may be overt (e.g., bowling leagues, sales records, grades) or covert, where you constantly compare yourself with others (with or without their knowing it). Competition is most enjoyable if the participants feel in control of their involvement. You don't feel this control. You feel a need to compete and com-

pare yourself with others. You are on a treadmill that may
slow down at times, but it doesn't stop. You can't find the
switch. This compulsive competition can bring out the worst
in you. It can make you an arrogant gossip or a bitter failure.
Win or lose, you never find the "off" switch. You never get
control.

You can imagine a better life. In your head you can see a
happier, healthier you. This feels good. So you spend time
here, in fantasy, daydreaming about the person you think
you should be. You probably keep these fantasies to yourself. Your closest friends may not know anything about them.
These daydreams make you feel good but, like many aspects
of yourself, you would be embarrassed if they were exposed.
Maybe you see yourself in love with the perfect person who
knows everything about you and still loves you unconditionally. Perhaps you see yourself succeeding in the career of your
choice. Your daydreams may be filled with riches but, more
importantly, they are filled with love, respect, appreciation,
applause, and caring. You use these daydreams to help you
through hard times.

You carry a destructive fantasy that will, sooner or later,
have to be corrected. You feel less than adequate because you
don't measure up to some ideal image of yourself that lives
in your head. This ideal image may have been created by you
or by your parents, your teachers, your coaches, society, or all
of the above and more. In any case, you have an image of
yourself that is so unreal (or, perhaps, so unlike you) that you
feel defective because the real you cannot match this. This
unrealistic image needs to go. Your goals must be within your
reach. Then, when you achieve those goals, you may want
to create a new destination. An idealized image of who you
need to be will only make who you are feel inadequate by
comparison.

But I don't expect this advice to be taken easily. You need to be that awesome person who lives in your imagination. You may tell yourself otherwise, but you do. In order to become this image, you have to be virtually perfect. If you decide you want to do something, you feel you must do it at an A+ level. Anything less would be a failure. B+ just isn't good enough. You are either a hero or a zero. In the back of your head and deep in your heart you hold on to the hope that perfection might bring you everything you need. Perfection might bring you love and respect, admiration, and power. The pursuit of perfection places pressure on you, so much pressure that it can kill much of the enjoyment of life.

Because failure is so painful and is also an inevitable experience, you've had to find a way to anesthetize the sting. You've probably developed several means to do so, but one of your favorite moves is simply not to try. In other words, if you cannot do something well, you tend not to do it at all. You may be an all-star on your softball team, but you won't even look at the instructions on how to prepare your income taxes. You stay with the things you can do well. You don't venture off into areas that might show everyone how imperfect you are. You start near the top or you don't start at all. This unwillingness to begin from a position of relative weakness and grow stronger and more competent, of course, stunts your growth. Actualizing your potential often means starting at the bottom. As someone once said, "The only way to learn French is to admit you don't know French."

You tend to divide yourself between worrying too much (perfectionism) and worrying too little (apathy). At your best, you focus on learning, accomplishing, and doing what's right. But there are too many times when you focus only on how you appear to others. Your priority is to keep the flaws from showing. You remain ever vigilant, lest they float to the surface and prove you incompetent. Hiding is the key. Honest self-expression takes a back seat.

You have urges to share more of yourself, but the risk is too great. You may have your share of long talks with friends; you may even be or have been in counseling. But it's doubtful you've disclosed all you need to. Real self-disclosure is difficult for you. Shame is the enemy of self-disclosure. Shame drives you to keep important parts of yourself tucked away. In the more severe forms of shame, this material may be buried so deeply that you may not know it is there. If you are dealing with a milder form, though, you are probably aware of what you keep suppressed. You realize that secrets are locked in your basement. You may turn away for periods of time, but, for the most part, you understand that there is more to you than people know.

This point may seem incidental, but it will become important when we begin to discuss healing. Self-disclosure is a crucial dimension of recovery. It is also one of the most difficult steps. It is too often the step where people turn around and go back into hiding. More on this later.

Making decisions poses a real challenge for you. Your decisions are a form of self-disclosure. They communicate a great deal about you. Furthermore, where there are decisions there is the potential for failure. You are constantly reminding yourself that you could make the wrong choice. Then you would be exposed as foolish or naive or whatever description you fear most. You depend too much on what other people think when it comes time to select an option. You don't have enough faith in your own conclusions. Your feelings don't have adequate input either. External forces, such as the opinions of others, decide your course. Consequently, if this condition continues or worsens, you may come to feel that you are living someone else's life. Even if, like the angry adolescent, you rebel against those who might control you by making decisions contrary to their preferences, those authority figures still control you. You will not have a mature identity until your decisions come from you, based on your own thoughts, feelings, and conscience. Then you will be living your own life.

Another factor that compromises your ability to decide is your energy. Shame is all about hiding, and hiding requires energy. It takes energy to force pieces of yourself into the dungeon. It takes even more energy to keep them there. This energy could be used to help build relationships, pursue enjoyable activities, and contribute to work that you find meaningful. But the more those submerged parts of you fight to be seen, the more energy you need to keep them below the surface. Another unfortunate cycle develops. Decreased energy decreases the chances of achieving desired outcomes. With fewer successes, the chances of overcoming your inadequacy dwindle. If you could free that energy, however, you might be able to improve your functioning in all areas of your life.

One final reason decisions, or any other type of self-disclosure, can be difficult for you concerns your inability to forgive yourself. When you make a mistake, the effects stay with you for an unreasonably long time. Much of the trouble stems from the fact that you don't feel you deserve forgiveness. You don't love yourself enough. Then there is the fact that you don't take the time to understand yourself. Understanding yourself is a necessary part of forgiving yourself. You may have read every self-help book ever written, but you still haven't read you. At least you haven't read the chapters that need the most attention.

The irony is that you probably don't have to forgive yourself for as many wrongs as you think. Who you are may not be so unforgivable. But you have to look and see and decide for yourself. To look is to begin to understand. To understand is to begin to forgive. Once you can forgive yourself, you will not be as frightened by your imperfection. Forgiven imperfection becomes humility. Unforgiven imperfection becomes shame.

The Russian author Tolstoy once wrote that "shame is an open wound." Some wounds are deeper than others. Earlier I suggested that shame is like an infectious disease that spreads through one's system. As such, mild shame can, and often does, deteriorate into a more severe form. People who are experiencing mild shame may be in the early phase of a tragic situation. Or they may be in the latter stages of healing.

There are at least three qualities present in the milder forms that more or less disappear should this condition progress. First, people at this level have an awareness of how they are feeling and, perhaps, why they feel that way. They have an almost heroic honesty. They live with an awareness of the discomfort rather than retreat into denial. Because they are honest about their pain, they develop a knack for recognizing this kind of struggle in others. Typically, they can empathize quite well. And even though they may have trouble meeting their own needs, they are often quite good at recognizing and tending to the needs of others. It was been my experience, in fact, that a lot of therapists—including some very effective therapists—suffer from this low-grade feeling of inferiority. This is not to say that they are functioning at their optimal level. This will not occur until the wound heals. But I am proposing that people with less than overwhelming feelings of inferiority can still function very well in certain areas. For the most part, they very much want to help, as well as gain the approval of others.

Second, they have hope. Inadequacy has trouble taking complete control as long as a person has hope. Hope combats despair. Hope delivers the message that better times may be ahead. "I may not be good enough now, but I may be some-day," whispers the hopeful soul. "If I'm damaged, I don't have to be damaged forever," it insists. The light at the end of the tunnel is the light that can reveal all the scenes and secrets that get hidden away to form the foundation of self-doubt. The light is fueled by hope. As the secrets are brought be-fore the light, healing begins. Hope is essential to the healing process.

Third, people who stop the spread of shame tend to be people who have, somehow, found support for themselves. Since they don't appreciate their own beauty and goodness, this support causes them some confusion. They can't fully grasp why people care or are willing to put up with all their limitations. In many cases, this care gets explained away with rationalizations such as, "They don't know the real me." In spite of this, they are capable of feeling gratitude for the support they receive. This gratitude may be their strongest connection with humanity. This support, even though they question if it is deserved, has a tremendously positive effect on those who cannot affirm and emotionally support themselves.

This support helps them be fair with others, a fairness they do not extend to themselves. People with mild to moderate degrees of shame do not necessarily assume that all people think poorly of them. They can easily understand when they are judged harshly, but they are also willing to accept (and be grateful for) those who are good enough to make an effort to value them.

People with lesser amounts of shame are aware of their discomfort and, generally, would like to do something about it. They may be uncertain about how to make the neces-sary changes. They will try to make life better for themselves but only if they believe their efforts will not lead to further ridicule, humiliation, or abandonment.

Moderate Shame

If you are suffering from moderate shame, your pain can be significant. Much of the time you are aware of your hurt, but you are, at times, capable of blocking it out of your consciousness. It doesn't go away; it's just temporarily out of sight and out of mind. To the extent that you remain aware of these feelings, you live on the milder side of the shame continuum. To the extent you are unaware, you spend your days on the more severe end.

Many of the consequences of moderate shame are extensions of those present in the mild form. Those with these stronger feelings of inadequacy have an even greater fear of ridicule, and self-disclosure will be all the more difficult. If you fall into this category, you are starved for appreciation, and yet you are a criticism magnet. You find flaws in your most flawless performances. You have difficulty being satisfied with your decisions, and you constantly compare yourself with others. You seem to lack the ability to forgive yourself, and you spend far too much time in escapist fantasy. You also waste excessive amounts of energy trying to force your true self into hiding. You are good at this. As a result, the world seldom sees the real you.

You've lost faith in the real you. You may blame your problems on those around you, but deep inside, you're sure it's you. You're convinced that the adversity you face in life is caused by your inferiority.

You are aware that your condition could deteriorate. As bad as it sometimes feels, there could be more suffering ahead. For instance, maybe the beauty or athleticism of your youth led people to applaud you without looking too deep inside. As time passes and the outer you loses some of its splendor, the inner you feels pulled to the surface. The inner you does not feel like an adequate replacement for what was a valued exterior. It's like the day after Halloween; people liked your costume and you don't want to put it away. You don't feel good about what might be revealed.

Many mental health professionals contend that when pain becomes great enough, people are driven to make changes in their lives. While this may be true for the majority of individuals, there are exceptions. Among the exceptions are those who feel inadequate. You are capable of living with a tremendous amount of suffering before you will consider getting help or making changes. Asking for help feels frightening, and if you tried to change, you could fail and be humiliated. Better to be safe and tormented.

While pain usually adds to one's incentive to change, if you have significant feelings of inadequacy, you may be stuck in the pain. You don't give yourself credit for all the heartache you've survived. You simply accept it with a phrase like, "This is just the way it is." Besides, you're certain you won't be able to improve yourself anyway.

The essence of mental health may be the ability to learn from experience. If you learn from experience, you are constantly learning from life. This means finding ways to get your needs met and learning how to avoid making the same mistakes over and over. It all sounds so simple, but you struggle with this. You are handicapped in this area because you refuse to look deeply enough into the hard times. You doubt your strength and overall competence. You fear that looking at failures and losses might overwhelm you. Your life is largely a series of unexamined issues. You don't want to admit it, but you repeat the same mistakes, sometimes again and again. These errors then serve as proof of your inadequacy.

The harder you throw these memories into your unconscious, the harder they bounce back. Keeping them repressed may be possible for a while, but it takes effort. Energy that could be used to build health and happiness is squandered in the attempt to hide that which needs to be revealed and studied. You learn from experience by examining your experience—all of your experiences, including the gut-wrenching kind.

Besides repression, another defense you probably depend upon is projection. Projection means you project your unwanted thoughts onto other people. For example, people filled with self-loathing understandably have a hard time living with this awareness. So they may project this belief onto others. Instead of living with the thought, "I can't tolerate my own presence," they turn this into "They hate me," or "They will never really care for me," or some derivation of this. "They" can be anybody or everybody. Projection places the hostility outside of you but, at the same time, it places you in a hostile world.

If you use projection, you are not being fair to people. You are turning good people into your enemies and critics, people who have no desire to hurt and who, given the opportunity, would be quite loving. You see more animosity than actually exists. The world becomes a mean and frightening place, not because of anything that goes on out there, but because of what goes on inside of you. If your feelings of self-loathing escalate and your use of projection increases, this could turn into paranoia—the relentless suspicion that no one likes you or that they might even be trying to punish you. As psychologist Gershen Kaufman points out, "Shame is a fertile breeding ground for paranoia."[8]

In spite of the distance you often build between yourself and the people in your life, you are aware of your need for love. This need has always been a part of your healthy core. It refuses to die or surrender its voice. You are eager for love but question if anyone could really love you. You are, however, willing to accept that there are those who may need you. You look for those who are needy enough to stay with you. You tell yourself, consciously or unconsciously, that this is the best you can do. You may be so happy to have someone need you that, for a while, it feels like love. But this feeling doesn't last.

Not only do you want to be loved, you want to love. But something gets in the way. You can need someone like a drowning person needs a life raft, but loving is more of a challenge. You may say, "I love you," but you're never sure if you're doing it right. It sounds weak to you. Actually, it's hard for you to express love because it's difficult for you to express yourself at all. You keep so much of yourself hidden. As a result, the love you have to give is buried, yet waiting to be released.

You don't love yourself either. This makes it all the more important that people approve of you. Without their approval, you would have nothing. You don't love your life. You would like to, but you don't have the energy or the gratitude. Should you find yourself starting to love something, you will also feel yourself beginning to heal. You see, love can be the first major casualty of shame, but it is also an essential part of the cure.

You feel weak and vulnerable, and yet you have a temper. This rage may be aimed at objects or other people or at yourself. These tantrums may be the closest thing to power you've ever known. And though you may feel guilty after these episodes, it's probably just a matter of time until another one comes along. It's not so much that you like these outbursts. They occur because you *need* them. Besides the power they bring, they serve to restore your faith that you really do have a store of feelings somewhere inside you. They also remind you of all the energy within, energy that may someday be used in healthy ways.

Most other times, you feel quite vulnerable. An open sore waiting to be prodded. In spite of all the hiding you do, you still feel unprotected. You are an underprotected person in an often hostile world. The world outside you is hostile and so is your internal world. Your inner self reminds you of your inadequacy by way of shaming thoughts. Sometimes called "automatic thoughts," these messages barge into your consciousness seemingly any time they like. You usually feel defenseless against them. Examples of these thoughts are: "You're not good enough." "They're better than you are." "They can all see how incompetent you are." "You're a mess." "Don't even try; you'll embarrass yourself."

Typically, these messages come a few sentences at a time and last only long enough to remind you how inferior you are. But for some people, these episodes can burst into full-blown shame attacks. In a shame attack, these awful accusations come from everywhere, all at once, and feel as though they'll never stop. The volume and intensity of the insults skyrockets. The attack, it seems, is not just an attempt to hurt you; it feels as if it wants to destroy you. And it does so by assaulting your future. A shame attack will tell you how terrible you are and how you will always be this way. It tries to remove all hope. If you have experience with shame attacks, you know that they do not last forever. To those dealing with their first few attacks, they can seem frighteningly permanent.

Unfortunately, we know very little about shame attacks. Those who have them are frequently too afraid or too shamed to reveal them. I believe people may be more prone to have them when their physical energy becomes depleted. Those who have trouble sleeping may be more vulnerable. They often come in the wee hours of the morning when a person is alone, tired, and without enough productive work to keep from ruminating. But people have had these attacks at all hours of the day and night. Shame attacks are quite dangerous, as they can lead to self-destructive behaviors.

In a way, whether or not you have out-and-out shame attacks, you are virtually always under attack. This is because you criticize yourself frequently, intensely, and destructively. The criticisms you make of yourself are not intended to correct and improve. Rather, they seek only to hurt and to punish. We all criticize ourselves from time to time. This is how we make adjustments and grow. With healthy self-criticism, we point ourselves toward opportunities for growth. For example, healthy self-criticism tells us to learn more, try harder, relax, or be more patient. Unhealthy self-criticism, on the other hand, simply snorts, "You're no good!" "You're a moron!" or "You'll never get it right!" This type of criticism only generates greater feelings of inadequacy. It doesn't point anywhere productive. At best, it keeps you stuck. More likely, it makes you feel worse.

In spite of the discouragement you fill yourself with, you have still had your successes, haven't you? You don't give yourself enough credit, but there have been times when you have risen above your own discouragement and showed yourself to be quite competent. It may well be that on some of these occasions, you still find a way to feel uncomfortable. In the wake of your most significant triumphs, you may feel like a fake. This is sometimes called the Impostor Syndrome. You don't feel like a success, so your accomplishments can't be real. They only *appear* real. Sooner or later your incompetence will show. It's only a matter of time. Until then, you live anxiously, perhaps grateful for the good luck and yet knowing that eventually you will lose it all. Then you will be exposed for what you feel you really are.

Your self-criticism is, most of the time, automatic. It comes on without much warning. It has its own key to your psyche. It doesn't have to be invited. The critical voice bursts into your consciousness seemingly at will. Somewhere along the line, you stopped fighting it. You surrendered unconditionally, and now the critical voice has become a tyrant. It impacts your thinking, but it does not yet control your behavior. With the critical voice whining away, you continue to struggle, putting one foot in front of the other. You may be on the verge of giving up (because your critical voice tells you that you will inevitably fail), but you don't always quit. To your credit, and with that discouraging voice jabbering in your head, you go to work or to school; you move ahead with the work you need to do. You can't seem to stop the voice, but the voice can't seem to stop you either. You are burdened but still moving. If your critical voice develops the power to control your behavior, you will be caught in the clutches of severe shame.

It's important to remember that you want to be a good, healthy person. You want others to like you, and you want to feel safe. You may not have much faith in any of these, but the desire still burns. You may go far out of your way to be of service to others. You do so for several reasons. You want people to approve of you. Beyond this drive for approval, you have a real desire to help people. But there's a third dimension to this. You live with the feeling that you owe people something. You're always in debt, a debt you never seem able to pay. Your contributions aren't enough. You should be doing more.

As feelings of inferiority increase, they influence more and more of a person's life. They color one's perception, beliefs, attitudes, and interpersonal relationships. They bias these dimensions in ways that sustain the inadequacy. This person sees, hears, and feels criticisms where there are none. She predicts humiliation without cause. In order to keep herself safe, she may make herself as unlikable as possible in an effort to keep people at a distance. She may humiliate herself, resorting to chronic complaining or other forms of hostility that serve to push people away. Beneath it all, there lives a genuine desire to be close to those she walls off.

At this level of shame, one of two paths may be taken. First, the condition may continue to deteriorate. The self-loathing builds to the point where it strangles the will to change. The person feels incapable of escaping the torment. Here the situation gets increasingly dangerous. Remember Adler's point that "No human being can bear a feeling of inferiority for long." Something must give. The pain becomes too great. Something must be done. The condition deteriorates when (a) the person blocks awareness by using denial, repression, and other defenses, or (b) the person becomes self-destructive.

In many ways, it is the natural progression of inferiority to build defenses. From the beginning, shame is about concealing. Thus it is not surprising that as it increases, it leads to severe levels of denial and repression. These defenses require energy—energy to keep more and more material pushed down into the unconscious. This energy could be used to laugh and learn, build and create. But instead it gets wasted, holding unacceptable feelings below the surface. If these defenses are surrendered, this energy becomes free to contribute to a healthy life. On the other hand, if it continues to be used to repress what should be expressed, the individual will become more or less exhausted. On the outside, he may appear lifeless. On the inside, enormous amounts of energy are being spent trying to keep his real self hidden. In short, all his energy is being spent, and he has little left to make a better life for himself.

As he loses faith in his ability to make a better life for himself, thoughts of suicide are possible. Ironically, sometimes it is their self-loathing that keeps people at this stage from killing themselves. They may not see themselves as deserving a better life after they're dead and may imagine themselves going to an even worse place. I have heard more than a few people with these feelings say, "I'd kill myself but I'd just end up in hell." So, fortunately, they stay alive. Unfortunately, many remain alive and miserable.

Then there is the other path. At this place that I am calling moderate shame, people are still aware of their feelings of inadequacy. They have the strength and courage to carry this burden and sometimes even maintain a little hope that life might get better someday. Still, the pain can be significant. And it is the awareness of this pain that can motivate positive change. People who are in touch with their discomfort have a reason and an impetus to seek comfort. Here lies another conflict. The pain says, "Change." The shame says, "Don't risk it; you'll fail." The anguish pushes people toward relief and health. The shame drives them toward repression and pathology. How this conflict is resolved will determine whether the person moves toward healing or toward a more severe form of shame.

Those who move into severe shame encounter a new enemy. People cannot maintain an awareness of this much pain. Their sense of inferiority rules their lives, but it is almost always in disguise. When shame reaches the point where it has the power to disguise itself, it can be a truly devastating and life-threatening condition.

Severe Shame

Severe shame is intolerable. No one can live well with this pain. At this level, your sense of inadequacy controls your past, present, and future. Your personal history appears filled with failures, losses, and humiliations. You can't see much else in your story. In the present, you are inferior, incapable, and defective. You may have a talent or two, but you consider them flukes that will soon be exposed as such. Your future has no hope. At best, everything will remain as is. More likely, your life will get worse.

This is "reality" if you suffer from this condition. But, of course, this reality is far too harsh to live with. You feel certain that this reality cannot change. So you either avoid the awareness of how defective you are or you destroy yourself. You will first try to deny your inadequacy. You put all you have into these defenses. If they should fail, self-destruction—either direct or indirect—will probably follow. This amount of pain, without the hope of relief, is simply intolerable.

If you carry this kind of shame, you may have tried a variety of defenses or you could be holding tenaciously to one. We have discussed projection, but at this stage the projection may be more like paranoia. You can't live with the animosity you feel for yourself. You take these feelings and project them onto others. Now your biases become (you believe) their conclusions. Now you may no longer feel hatred toward yourself, but you feel hostility coming from those around you. Your world is now filled with critical judges. To most people, this wouldn't sound like much of an improvement. But this is a choice you make (though perhaps unconsciously). You know that nothing is worse than self-hatred. You can sometimes hide from others' hostility. Hostility that you feel for yourself, however, would follow you into every hiding place.

Perfectionism is another defense. If you use perfectionism to deal with severe shame, though, you are using major league perfectionism. Failure, any kind of failure, is unbearable because it proves to the world how horrible you are. You don't just *prefer* to be perfect, you absolutely need to be. Mistakes may lead to major psychological consequences such as deep depression. Terrible rage is also common, rage that if directed toward others may even be homicidal or if directed toward yourself could lead to suicidal thoughts. Underneath all this is a small, frightened, wonderful inner child who is still hoping that if she does everything perfectly, she will be loved.

The intensity you put into your perfectionism may have made you quite successful. But you probably don't feel successful. At best you feel relieved because you've made it through another day without your awfulness being exposed. You have fooled them for one more day. Your perfectionism is your myth of personal perfection. And if you practice it long enough and hard enough, you may actually come to convince yourself that you are flawless. As long as you can force yourself to believe you are perfect, you can avoid the truth.

This is one of the most common defenses against powerful feelings of inferiority. Narcissism, the belief that one is more special than the rest, has been described as the ultimate defense against shame. If you use a narcissistic defense to deal with your inadequacy, you've created a delusion of specialness. Your imagination has become your identity. You present yourself as something you are not. In fact, you present yourself as quite the opposite of what, deep inside, you really believe you are. You are no longer inferior. Instead, you are clearly superior. You tend to ridicule others' shortcomings and you look to surround yourself with people who believe you are everything you say you are. You love being around folks who say "Wow!" at the sight of you. You have little empathy or sympathy for another person's insecurities, because getting too close to human pain might trigger an awareness of what's really going on inside of you. Should anyone suggest to you that your arrogance is based in self-contempt, you will reject this outright. Your shame is now beneath your awareness (unless you've begun to heal, in which case your pain may be starting to surface).

You may be aware of humiliations in your life, but you insist that you've risen above them and may even degrade those who express pain for having experienced similar ordeals. You don't want to feel. You won't allow yourself to feel. Feelings are too honest, and they don't tolerate defenses well. If you allow yourself to feel, honesty may take over. Because honesty seems intolerable, you separate yourself from your feelings. People who use a narcissistic defense can't risk feeling. It could start an avalanche of awareness that could, they believe, lead to a breakdown. Narcissists resent their feelings because there is no way to feel perfectly. Feelings are beautifully flawed. Just like human beings.

If you use a narcissistic defense, you insist upon being wonderful. No flaws allowed. You present yourself as completely self-confident without reason to ever doubt yourself. You live your life to protect this facade. This facade must be convincing enough to fool others and yourself. It must be so convincing that no one, including you, suspects the mayhem that lies underneath it. Should the facade crack and expose all those concealed flaws, you are faced with an experience that may feel genuinely overwhelming.

Among the costs of these defenses is the loss of self-awareness. You never get to know yourself. You spend your energy preventing this from occurring. You assume that everything you fear about yourself is true. You no longer challenge these fears. You simply accept them (and surrender to them) as accurate.

Besides the fact that you've not been introduced to yourself, you are lonely. If you enter into relationships at all, you will only stay in them until the other person is beginning to see the real you. At this point, you will either end the relationship or change your behavior in a way that pushes that person away. Whatever approach you use, you will leave behind you a string of people who once cared for you who are left to wonder, "What went wrong?" Sadly, they may never know.

The envy that exists in mild and moderate levels of shame is magnified in you. There is almost always someone to fire your jealousy. Envy arises when one person resents feeling inferior to another. You feel inferior to just about everyone. Not only do you feel inferior, you feel intensely inferior. You will never be comfortable with this. No one ever gets used to feeling inferior. It always hurts. Whenever projection, narcissism, or your other defenses stop working, jealousy will typically follow. No defense works perfectly, so there will inevitably be periods of envy.

This is not at all like petty jealousy. When envy becomes intense, as it does if you have strong feelings of inadequacy, it seeks to destroy those who cause you to feel inferior. In most cases this destruction comes in the form of gossip or slander. But it is also a common cause of physical violence.

You would like to be close to people, but you can't seem to make it happen. It's hard for you to say, "I love you." The calluses that have formed around your wounds have kept the love out. You may see love around you, but you don't *feel* it. You can't give what you don't have. But you try to love. You want to love. You want to feel love. You crave love. You feel the void and it torments you.

This is one of the most devastating consequences of shame's lies: you feel too inadequate to give and receive love. You are most certainly capable of touching and sharing love, but you won't believe this. If your feelings of shame have reached this level, you not only feel unlovable, you also feel unable to really love anyone. You feel capable of needing someone, but not of loving someone. Loving means giving. You seldom feel you have anything of value to give.

You may have found a partial solution that helps you survive. You may, for instance, allow yourself to love and feel love from animals. Because you have more control over animals, there is less chance of being hurt. Or you may have shallow relationships that are primarily sexual in nature that give momentary relief. Or you may allow yourself to love your creations. I have known a number of shame-filled individuals who have used their art to keep their love alive. In many of these people, their creativity is the only part of their psyches left unconquered by shame.

Shame, however, grows. If nothing slows its development, it becomes a dominating force. When this occurs, your defenses are no longer effective. You can no longer pretend to be perfect. You don't have the energy or the confidence to maintain that facade. When shame takes control, projection collapses. It dawns on you that the reason people don't like you is that you are unforgivably flawed. It's not them. It's you. And the worst you could believe about yourself feels accurate.

At this point, in another attempt to relieve your pain, you look for distractions. But shame has so much control that even your distractions are shameful. You may indulge in unusual sexual behavior, anything to get your mind off yourself. Since shame is now making most of your decisions, however, you select behaviors that will, ultimately, shame you. I have known people in this condition who have cut themselves repeatedly, forced themselves to vomit, exposed themselves, eaten repulsive substances, and picked at sores until they became infected. These behaviors can be faulty attempts to take the focus off the pain that dwells within.

The distractions are rarely effective enough to keep away thoughts of suicide. Even if you are secure in the conviction that you would never take your life, you still have these thoughts. You wonder about it. What it might do. How it might feel. But no matter how hard things get, you are never convinced that destroying yourself is the right decision. There is always (and will always be) a part of you fighting for life. This is a part of your healthy core that you refuse to acknowledge. Psychologist Edwin Schneidman, widely considered the leading authority on the subject of suicide, has written, "I have never known anyone who was one hundred percent for wanting to commit suicide."[9] Health always accounts for at least a few percentage points.

Here, though, is one of the greatest dangers in the process of recovering from severe shame. In order to heal, you must first become aware. You have to become aware of what you are dealing with. You must realize the self-loathing and understand what it is doing to your life. This awareness, although healthy in the long run, can be overwhelming at first. It is here, I'm afraid, where many suicides occur. The awareness of strong feelings of inadequacy may feel like the final breakdown. In truth, this could be the first step in an enormous breakthrough. As illogical as it may sound, many people end their lives as their condition is actually improving. The situation is particularly dangerous when someone feels inferiority without hope. Hope can carry one through the bad times. Without it, there may appear to be little reason to fight the good fight.

Shame is usually, if not always, a part of suicide. Shame is the pain that fuels the act. People don't kill themselves to escape to something. They destroy themselves to escape *from* something. That something is typically the conscious or unconscious belief in their own defectiveness. Even when the belief lives only in the unconscious, it can still be lethal. But these people have less of an understanding of why they are ending their lives.

If you have lived with this much discomfort, you may

also be engaging in what has been called "chronic suicide."
This means a person repeatedly participates in self-destructive
behaviors such as drug use, reckless driving, or excessive
drinking. Alcohol abuse is a particularly popular form of
chronic suicide in our culture. And although excessive drinking can indeed be fatal, it does have at least one benefit.
Psychiatrist Donald Nathanson suggests that "alcohol seems
to work as a shame killer."[10] While you are intoxicated, you
may feel free from that nagging sense of inadequacy. Some
people find this to be the case while others do not. Your shame
may be alcohol-proof. And those who receive comfort from
alcohol soon learn that this comfort is only temporary. After
the drink wears off, the shame comes back to life—usually
stronger than ever.

You don't want to feel the pain. When the pain and everything else you try to hide move to the surface, you feel
desperate. You can't live with the feelings you have toward
yourself. The key to survival (at least at first) is, of course,
hope. Hope helps you look at yourself for the purpose of
improving what you need to improve and accepting what
you need to accept. This hope is the first step in healing
shame.

If you do not yet feel any hope, you will probably continue
to live with defenses, distractions, and self-destructiveness.

The experience of severe shame is difficult to articulate.
This is one of the reasons those with this condition find it so
hard to get people to understand them. Even after they begin
to open up, their stories are often difficult to comprehend. It
doesn't make sense that people would hold so tenaciously to
their self-hatred. Yet, if you listen closely enough, the pieces
usually come together. Shame is not a detail of one's life. It
is a theme. As such, to understand it, you must look at the
broader picture of a person's life.

Michael, for example, has spent virtually his entire life try-ing to free himself from an overwhelming sense of his own inadequacy. He has lived in a variety of places and has tried hard to make his life happy. An intelligent man, Michael has had some success at happiness, but it has been fleeting. He has not been able to find or create the life he would like to live.

Michael has had a long series of physical ailments, most of which appear to have been psychosomatic. He has been called "a classic hypochondriac," and there could be some truth to this. But this does not diminish at all the pain he has lived with. He is filled with stories and feelings that need to be shared. He uses his body, however, to constantly remind people, "There's something wrong with me." When he began therapy, he could only tolerate sharing the possibility that his body might be defective. Now, as he is becoming stronger and more hopeful, he is starting to share his feelings of inadequacy related to the rest of his being.

I am using Michael as an example because he is at the point in his recovery where he can most accurately describe the monster. He is now looking right at it. All those aspects of himself that were too horrible to expose are now reaching the light of day. He is facing the fear of what will happen now that his secrets are being released. There may come a day when he no longer focuses on his inadequacy. But right now, he has the best seat in the house to see and describe severe shame.

"The first time I felt good about me was when I got drunk for the first time at eleven." His childhood was one long string of reminders that showing emotion is wrong, especially for boys. Michael was an emotional child prone to showing and sharing his feelings, but he learned that being who he was was "wrong." As often happens, Michael began to see the same message sent from different sources. He once told me, "I was only allowed two feelings—anger and laughter." As he realized this, I'm sure he figured he might never belong anywhere.

Interestingly, Michael's mother was a nurse and, as such, she was willing to respond to her children's physical needs. His father had chronic physical disabilities, which added a greater acceptance to the expression of physical pain. In this family, physical pain was tolerated. Emotional pain was not. Michael learned the rules. He carried the memories of his parents telling him they would leave him if he didn't stop crying.

Michael says he's "always afraid that I'm not going to measure up." He fears being "less than human" and "less than good." He says he feels like a "five-year-old" who constantly has "a grown-up standing over me saying 'bad, bad, bad!'" This grown-up never goes away and never smiles, hugs, or shows any sign of approval.

Michael also tells me, "I was supposed to be brave, strong, and able to tackle anything on my own. If not, I was not a real human being." It is important to note that Michael is an intelligent, educated, and, in many ways, successful man. Of course, he does not describe himself using many positive terms. In fact, he indicates that, for most of his life, he has believed that if anyone discovered how awful he really is, he would die. His inferiority had convinced him that "if anyone knew the real me, it would kill me!"

Because he concealed so much of himself, Michael lived a lonely life. "I have kept people away most of my life," he says with downcast eyes. If people get too close, they might see all the terrible secrets. They might see that he has feelings. So he keeps his emotions tucked away. He doesn't want to be shamed, abandoned, or killed. He wants to be loved. He just can't bring himself to tell anyone. Besides, he convinced himself long ago that he is not worthy of love.

I'm not sure what will become of Michael. He has many gifts and he seems willing to begin accepting them. He has had the strength to keep himself alive through the darkest nights. He holds tightly to a faith in God, a God who is becoming more loving as time passes. His secret feelings are being revealed gradually, and thus the energy that was being used to repress them is now being used in more positive ways. But, more than anything, the reason I hope for Michael is that Michael is beginning to hope for himself.

Another example is Kate. Kate was the star in her family. She surpassed her four brothers in every arena in which she chose to compete. She was the better student, athlete, and musician. Growing up, she was more popular than they and seemed to have the brightest future. But now, at age thirty-nine, she is not at all what she was "supposed to be."

Kate never felt as good as the persona she presented. She believed she had to be the family hero, but as time passed she felt more and more like a failure. She couldn't keep the pace. No matter how well she did, it seemed the people around her always expected more. To her, exhaustion meant failure, so she masked her fatigue. She could only press on.

Through her adolescence, she was too perfect for anyone to worry about. But she didn't enter her twenties well. She dropped out of college and bounced between jobs. To those who knew her, it was just a matter of time before she would hit her stride again. Kate, however, was becoming increasingly convinced that she had lost her stride forever. Upon turning thirty, her anxiety increased. She feared that she might never marry or have children. The fear became so great that it started making her decisions for her.

She decided to marry a man with whom she had little

in common. He was, by everyone's estimation, including his own, an underachiever who had little to offer Kate. They now have two daughters and live in a cold and lifeless marriage. He feels Kate demands too much of him. Kate harbors resentment because she feels he provides a poor role model for their children. Still, neither seriously considers divorce.

In spite of the distance between them, Kate needs this man. Deep inside, she cannot forgive herself for not living up to the impossible standards that were set for her early in life. Her family needed a hero, and she could be nothing less. As they say, she could be a hero or a zero. Because she could not manage to remain a hero as an adult, she became the disappointment who (she believes) let her family down. She lost faith in her ability to rise above inadequacy. The best she could do was (a) create distractions for herself, and (b) provide an explanation for her failings. Unwittingly, her husband served both these purposes. This man became her (and her family's) excuse as to why she is not living up to everyone's ideal. In other words, her failings are his fault (so this story goes). Beyond this, her ongoing marital conflict serves to distract her from the pain she feels over falling short or becoming the person she still thinks she needs to be.

Kate and her husband have now come to marital therapy to help improve their marriage. Right now, however, the prognosis is poor. Neither wants to change. Each insists that the other has "the problem" and needs to change. If they can begin to honestly look at themselves, the prognosis may improve.

When shame becomes severe enough, people stop asking, "How can I get better?" and start asking, "How can I live with this?" They lose the hope needed to heal and settle for learning to cope with an inevitable and ongoing torment. Shame can be healed, but when it grows to a certain size it can strangle hope. People then stop looking for health and, instead, focus on finding ways to survive while living miserable lives.

Both Kate and Michael, and everyone else who feels grossly inadequate, have been caged by hopelessness. Think of their situation this way: *If there is no hope, there is no hope. If there is hope, there is hope.* The good news is that hope is always possible. Someone saturated with shame begins to heal with the arrival of hope. To get started in recovery, one only needs enough hope to honestly state, "Maybe I can be good enough."

Chapter Three

Healing: The Basics

Our first rule: Start by being gentle with yourself. During the course of the next two chapters, I will not ask you to do anything nearly as difficult as what you have been doing to yourself. You already know how to brutalize yourself. It's true that recovery from a condition as serious as this often requires a kick in the pants to keep going. But, face it, you've been kicking yourself all over for longer than you can remember. You know how to kick. Now you need to care for yourself.

Speak to yourself gently. Show respect. A survivor like you deserves it. Disrespect has crippled you. Respect will strengthen your walk and gently push you in healthier directions. Address yourself with "please" and "thank you" and "I'm sorry" and "you're welcome." Open your fists and lift your head. Look yourself and others in the eye. Even if this does not yet feel natural, practice it.

We are going to move in small steps, and you will control the pace. When you stop and start will be up to you. But please do not let fear make your decisions. Keep control of your decision making. Do what you know is right. You have everything you need to make good decisions. And even on those occasions when you make a bad decision, you are strong enough to apologize, and make the needed corrections, and survive.

The changes you need to make are probably not nearly as

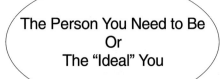

many as you think. People with low self-esteem often believe that in order to be accepted, loved, and appreciated, they will have to completely reinvent themselves. If they try to improve themselves, they often look for gurus capable of altering their very soul and DNA. Small changes, they conclude, are not nearly enough. They are too defective to benefit from small alterations. If you feel this way, the future looks pretty bleak. What you need to do seems far beyond what you are capable of doing.

You need to start by reexamining these goals. Don't even think about changing one hundred percent of yourself. That is neither possible nor necessary. In round numbers, we're probably looking to change about ten or possibly fifteen percent of you. That's all. The rest we will keep, at least for now. Other aspects of yourself will change as you age, but for now we don't want to change more than fifteen percent. The rest of you is fine for now. Indeed, one of the most significant changes we need to make is to have you accept the majority of you. So, don't try to change too much. This would be setting yourself up for failure.

Keep in mind that the reason you feel you're not good enough is that the image you carry of the person you believe you have to be is not at all like the image you have of yourself. The two images are represented on the facing page. We need to bring these images closer together. Although there is always room for growth, and healthy people are aware that they would like to improve themselves, the discrepancy between the two images must be manageable. Your goals should be real yet flexible. But you don't need to be perfect by tomorrow. In other words, the images should overlap without being identical:

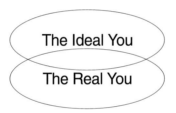

We must deal with the discrepancy between who you are and who you feel you need to be by addressing both images. Both images may need to change. The ideal you may need to become more realistic. The real you may need to grow. You need to look at both and ask some important questions. Who and what do you really need to be? Are your goals realistic? Is that ideal image a creation of someone who never really understood you? Is that ideal image a form of perfection that can never be attained? Is that image a set-up for failure? And even if you achieved this goal, would you be happy with your life?

Then there's the image you have of the person you are now. Who else sees you the same way? Could you be wrong?

Could this image be more negative than real? Does this image you have of yourself contain any strengths? If so, what are they? Can this image grow and change, or do you see it as stuck? Can it change a little? That's all we need right now. Just enough change to get you unstuck. You need these two images moving closer together.

With these thoughts in mind, we can proceed on the road to healing. In the basics of recovery, you will need to grow in five areas: hope, human contact, revealing your story, owning your pain, and forgiveness. You are capable of developing all these qualities. Start slowly. Respect yourself. Be gentle.

Hope

Hope is the beginning. Your future starts to brighten when you accept the full range of what is possible. This is what you need at this point: the freedom to consider the possible. Consider the possibility that your life can be more than it is right now, that it could contain more love, more happiness, more hope than it has. Hope is the willingness to consider the positive possibilities.

What often gets lost is the fact that hope is a choice. We decide whether or not we will include hope in our lives. It's not a gift that someone hands to us. Rather, it is a gift we give ourselves. We decide how we will look at the future. We may choose to see an endless string of dark clouds, or we can lift those clouds and allow the sun to break through. We can do this by ourselves. We cannot completely control our futures. But we can control our hope for the future. Hope is a choice. So is hopelessness.

Your past may influence your view of the future. You may be carrying scars, but they are probably not visible to the world. Your bad times do not own the road ahead of you.

Your memories do not control anything but what you allow them to. You do not have to be damaged goods forever. Give your imagination enough freedom, and you will begin to see how beautiful your life can be. You may be quick to criticize your first hopeful images. This criticism is an old pattern that will break in time. Persist right through the criticism. Allow hope to linger for a while. See it. Feel it. Try to get used to it. Remember, you choose your images of the future. Everyone's future has room for hope.

In your images of hope, include the skills you feel you have. Skills like listening, sewing, drawing, learning, exercising. Then add all the things you *could* do. These qualities include hidden talents that you've suspected you have but have never really put to use. Imagine these hidden talents blossoming. Ask yourself, "What would my future be like if I actually used all my talents?" Again, your first reaction may be to criticize. But stay with it. This pattern of self-criticism is destroyed as you practice hope. As the critic inside you becomes less of a tyrant, you will be freer. You may even develop the ability to affirm yourself.

Hope is more than a daydream. Hope has a power that simple daydreams lack. Most people with low self-esteem have indulged themselves in ongoing daydreams. Often these daydreams consist of stories where the dreamer emerges as the hero. These are in sharp contrast to the dreams they have at night where they find themselves humiliated and exposed as unprepared or inadequate. The daydreams may be so pervasive that they replace the need to achieve. Why risk trying to do it (in which case you could fail) when you can safely daydream about it? Daydreams seldom motivate. More often, when people who feel inferior daydream, their daydreams keep them glued to their inferiority.

Hope, on the other hand, motivates us to achieve. It pulls

us to make our dreams come true. But hope itself is not a dream. It describes what our lives could be if we worked hard and made the right choices. Hope pulls us to act. It lures us to emerge and rise above our circumstances. We choose hope, but then hope inspires us.

Hope teaches us that the past does not own the future. Hope looks you in the eye and says, "You don't have to feel bad about yourself!" As hope builds, the bars on your cell begin to disappear. You are no longer imprisoned by a defeatist attitude that insists, "Things will never change!" Your life *can* change! And you are in control of much of that change. You begin that change by choosing to hope.

It may help to look at other people's lives. If it's difficult to see your life improving, consider the truth that other people have changed their lives. This may open the door to possibility. People can change. Hold on to this. People do change. When your inner critic chimes in with, "Other people can change, but you can't," stay with it. Practice breaks the pattern of self-criticism.

I can tell you that many people who are filled with self-hatred turn their lives around and become healthy, self-loving human beings. Of course, there are others who will not. The two groups begin to distinguish themselves upon deciding whether or not to bring hope into their lives. Those who open themselves to the possibility that "things might get better" take that essential first step toward improving their lives.

Practice hope.

Human Contact

Your recovery will include other people. But before you close the book, please, read a little further. I know this may be a huge step in your healing process. You can, however, make it. Even if your life experiences indicate otherwise, there are people you can trust. People who will listen and care. People with flaws like everyone else, yet more than willing to reach out to a sincere request for help. Asking for help can be frightening. Still, it is a survival skill we all must learn.

Before you choose the people you would like to make a part of your recovery and your life, you are entitled to look around a little. Look at the people you already have in your life and decide which of those you would be willing to share more of yourself with. You may decide you want to connect with a clergyman, a counselor, or a support group. You will need more than one person in your life. With only one person, you would be tempted to place too many expectations on that single individual. Don't expect one person to fill all your interpersonal needs. Besides, it's not fair to place this many demands on one person. It's best to find at least a few people whom you choose to trust.

One good place to start is to find a doctor you feel comfortable with. A good physical examination performed by someone you trust can be very helpful at this point. Psychologically, it can be quite helpful to feel you have your doctor in your corner. Beyond this, you need to know if there are any medical issues that could be contributing to how you feel. There are a number of possibilities, not the least of which is depression. Depression and shame are separate conditions, but they often exist at the same time. One reason for this is that low self-esteem frequently leads to depression. Your doctor may recommend antidepressant medication which, if properly supervised, can be helpful. Medication does not cure feelings of inadequacy, but it may lift your energy enough to help you do the work necessary to feel better about yourself. In any case, if you are willing to risk the self-exposure needed to have your doctor understand what you have been through, you may be able to experience some immediate relief. The lesson is simple: the monster you have feared so much (i.e., self-revelation) will be a fundamental part of your healing.

You can surely list dozens of reasons not to reach out to people. Most of these probably center on the potential for being hurt. Another valid reason is that you've had little practice with this. New experiences can be frightening—not because you are weak but because you are human. In order to get the practice you need, you will have to walk through your fear. Learn from each experience, and your practice will be productive.

There are valid reasons to fear deep and genuine human contact. In your case, though, you have at least one other cause for concern, and it relates to the nature of shame. Your disclosures about your feelings of inadequacy will be unsettling for some people. If what you have to say causes them to recall or reexperience their own shameful memories, you may find them unwilling to listen. And because shame is typically hidden, you may be left with no apparent reason why you were turned away. Even some professional therapists are guilty of this. They've not worked through their own sense of inferiority, and thus cannot bring themselves to hear this struggle in others.

The risks are real. It makes no sense to pretend otherwise. But the risks are worth it. You can make deeper connections with people. You can learn to trust. The biggest roadblock to trust comes from within you. You may have many acquaintances, but you are reluctant to take your relationships any further than that. Someone might see how inadequate you are. You approach other people just like Charlie Brown did when he remarked, "I'd like to go talk with the little red-haired girl. But I can't because she's a somebody and I'm a nobody." It's hard to develop a deeper connection with people because they might discover exactly that, that you're a nobody. But if you get past the fear of being exposed as worthless, you realize something else about yourself. You will find that you are afraid of letting people see how afraid you are. You're sure they will completely overlook your courage and see only weakness. You focus on your flaws and look right past your strengths. You mistakenly assume that everyone else does too.

You must bridge the gap between yourself and the human community. In her book *On Shame and the Search for Identity,* Helen Lynd correctly points out, "The very fact that shame is an isolating experience also means that if one can find ways of sharing and communicating it, this communication can bring about closeness with other persons and with other groups."[11] People with low self-esteem live torn between the fear of closeness and the desperate need for closeness. When the fear is overcome, the need is fulfilled. It's doubtful that anyone could hurt you as much as you've been hurting yourself.

People who feel inferior frequently miss the potential for human connection that already exists in their lives. Maybe it's that person sitting in the room with you as you read this. It could be family members whom you've managed to keep at a distance. Feelings of inadequacy cause a type of blindness that keeps you from seeing the opportunities for good, healthy human contact. You may be socially adept—at a shallow level—but you don't get close and you don't get deep. Psychiatrist Andrew Morrison makes this point succinctly: "Connection with a loving, respecting spouse or friend can challenge a conviction of unworthiness and thus help dislodge shame."[12] But the blindness can cause you to overlook people who might want more than anything to get close to you. To remedy this, you must make a conscious decision to look for people to include in your life, people with whom you are willing to risk sharing yourself.

I say "people" because you might be tempted to go only part of the way and place all your needs on a single person. You might rationalize this by telling yourself something like, "The fewer the people who get near me, the less chance of getting hurt." While there might be some truth to this, all in all, it's faulty thinking. Demanding that one person meet all your needs is really just another version of isolation. Now you have two people hidden away. Many times, these types of relationships are made up of two shame-based people, both trying to arrange for some human contact with the least effort and the least risk. Two people willing to settle for any port in a storm. Besides, expecting one person to meet all your interpersonal needs places a tremendous amount of pressure on that individual. So much pressure that s/he may not want to stay in the relationship at all. There is no precise number that applies to all people. Some people survive quite well with a small group of close relationships, while others seem to need a larger group. But in just about all cases, one is not enough. You need to push yourself a little further than that.

Shame is all about the experience of isolation. It may help to be connected with your work or your pets or your art or music. None of these, however, will ever fill the need for human contact. You need to humble yourself enough to accept that you need people and empower yourself enough to start reaching out. Often the biggest step forward is the awareness of the need. When you feel poorly about yourself you may try to deny your need for people. Once this denial is broken, good things are more likely to occur.

Awareness is key. Awareness of your need for human contact as well as the awareness of what you have done to keep this need from being filled. You have kept people at a distance, and you may not realize how you have done it. You may have used a variety of techniques, or you may have a favorite move. A popular approach is the use of hostility to keep others away. This hostility can manifest itself in sarcasm, smugness, or aggressiveness. When someone gets too close, hostility finds some kind of expression. If you use hostility to isolate yourself, you are forever creating reasons to justify your anger. These reasons often center on the belief that you are provoked. This pattern continues until you become aware of it and begin taking responsibility for these choices.

Another common tactic is to belittle yourself. If this is your move, you wear a sign that informs people of how inadequate you are. You direct your hostility toward yourself. Although at first this may actually draw people to you, inevitably it has just the opposite effect. No one who might care for you wants you to degrade yourself. They don't want to stand by helplessly, unable to help you. You may call this tactic "honesty," or suggest that it hurts no one but you. You may not be aware that its true purpose is to keep people away. You're not doing it for the sake of honesty. You belittle yourself to keep yourself isolated. You don't see yourself; you devalue yourself.

A third common strategy is to alternate between hostility toward others and self-recrimination. If you use this approach, you push and pull. You push people away with your vindictiveness and pull yourself down with your self-abuse. This strategy is more complex than the singular approaches, but it is quite popular and effective (in an unhealthy kind of way). It can build a thick wall around you. To destroy the wall, you must recognize your behaviors for what they are and accept responsibility that you are the person maintaining them.

Recognize how you've pushed people away. Counseling may help with this. A trained professional may be able to spot what you have missed. You need to be aware when you are pushing people away. You need to see it clearly enough to stop and say to yourself, "Look at me! I'm doing it again!" I repeat, you need to be aware of how you keep others from getting close to you and you must take responsibility for this. This behavior has always been your choice. Your interpersonal skills may not be nearly as bad as you have thought. You have always been able to get people to do what you have wanted—stay away. Keeping people at a distance the way you have takes a certain skill. Now I'm suggesting that it's time you used your interpersonal skills to face the fear and move closer to people.

It might seem that a person who feels alone and isolated would move toward people like a person on fire would run toward water. And while the pain and desire are there, the movement toward cure may not be. In order to be good enough in your own eyes, you will have to find people to love. You will have to find people to reach out to and care for. You don't need to wait for the world to change. You have to let good people close enough to see inside you.

Tell Your Story

Your story. The story of your life. It must be told. The secrets have to be revealed. The locks have to be opened and the hinges need to be oiled. What has been hidden must be shared. What has been feared must be faced. It's time to be honest with yourself and those who would be close to you. It's time to introduce yourself to yourself. It's time to introduce yourself to the people who think they know you.

I'm *not* suggesting that you throw away your boundaries and tell everything to everyone. It's not that simple. To just let it all hang out without discretion can be damaging. You are entitled to privacy, and how you tell your story and with whom you will share it are major life decisions that must be weighed carefully.

The thought of telling your story probably stirs several emotions within you. The first to surface may be fear. You have made a life of keeping secrets. You've feared that if these secrets were revealed, you would be exposed as inadequate. These secrets may involve experiences in your life or thoughts in your head. Even if you've tried to tell your story in the past, you've kept some of this material hidden. This material may be repressed in your unconscious, leaving you with a nagging thought that there's more to your story but you just can't name it. The fear keeps getting in the way. So you keep these stories hidden.

In spite of the fear, you also feel an eagerness. You want to tell your full story. You want people to hear about your life. You would like to know for certain whether or not others could accept the real you. Your fear says they won't, but your hope says maybe, just maybe, they will. You would love to release the energy you waste keeping so much of yourself hidden. Maybe you've been told you are defective but there's a part of you that has been holding out for a second opinion. In fact, your inner desire to tell your full story has been so strong that it has actually added to your anxiety. You fear that some day this desire will become strong enough to rule the day and you will start disclosing all those concealed parts of you. And then what?

Thus far fear has controlled hope. But this can change. You see, if you decrease the fear, you increase the hope. The best way to manage fear is by making good decisions. If you fear that honest self-disclosure will cause you to be hurt, make the decision to look for people who aren't likely to hurt you. As you tell more and more of your story, you will have to choose your audience carefully. Look for those who might understand. People who refuse to tell their stories tend to use the same worn out line, "No one understands." They almost automatically put themselves in the role of victim. The truth is that there are people who will understand. It's your job to find them.

While telling your story to other human beings is essential to your recovery, you can practice on your own. Writing a journal about your life can be a good place to start. Write your story with a special emphasis on those areas you fear most. Open the locked doors. Look long and hard at what you see. Describe it in detail and give names to all the pieces. Explain your feelings, past and present. Some people use poetry to convey their emotions most effectively. If words are inadequate, draw pictures or write music. It might help to read your words aloud or speak them into a tape recorder. Listening to your own voice may, by itself, unlock a few doors.

Newly opened doors stir feelings. These new feelings may guide you. The sadness that makes it hard for you to speak asks you to listen to what you are feeling. The anger that causes your heart to pound reminds you of your strength and how much life you have within you. The hurt you feel tells you that you have the courage to feel pain—your own and that of others. Guilt implies your conscience has a healthy voice. Happiness reconfirms that life is worth living. Passion proclaims that there are causes worth fighting for. Loneliness insists that you keep looking for people to trust.

Practice telling the story of your real self, not that idealized image that you've felt you had to be. Every time you share a piece of that story you make your real self more real. Every time you reveal another aspect of your true self, your feelings of inadequacy slowly diminish. Shame survives through secrecy. As the secrecy is conquered, so is the shame.

Sooner or later you must tell your story to other human beings. This will not, nor should it, occur overnight. Your life is too deep and too rich to be summarized succinctly. You tell your story in pieces. For a while you may tell different pieces to different people. You may, for instance, share certain stories with your parents and others with your best friend. You may share a part of your life with your pastor and another part with your brother. In time, as you continue to self-disclose, each of these people may learn what each of the others know. The more you share, the closer you get. The closer you get, the more you share.

It takes time to tell your story. It also requires a great deal of courage. Your challenge will be to release your secrets. You need to unburden yourself. This may be your greatest challenge. But it will not be your only challenge. Just as you need to achieve balance in your life, you must look for balance in your personal history. Your tragedies, for instance, may outweigh your triumphs, but it is necessary to give recognition to your moments of joy. Many people who feel inadequate only look at their pain. Consequently, their memories comprise one long list of sorrows. They focus on their failures, losses, and weaknesses. Reciting your own personal list of heartaches is not telling your story. Rather, it is another attempt at belittling yourself for the purpose of keeping yourself safe and shamed. Over the years, I have worked with many, many people who have endured tremendous suffering, but I've never met anyone completely without positive experiences in their lives. A personal history that omits the good times is as incomplete as one that refuses to acknowledge the pain.

To recover from shame, you must learn to be fair with yourself. Start by being fair in the way you tell your story. If your history is only a list of hurts and mistakes, this may be an indication that you've not yet given yourself permission to be strong and contented. It also suggests that you have not yet become aware of your own life's story.

Jesse, a patient of mine in her early forties, exemplifies this. Married for almost twenty years and the mother of three healthy sons, she has many accomplishments to her credit. A competent physical therapist and former athlete, she has long been active in important community projects. She has friends and an extended family living nearby. Still, she reports having felt inadequate for a long, long time. A full range of psychiatric medications have been tried with minimal success. Her suffering would be virtually invisible to others except for her anger outbursts that occur a few times a year and only in the presence of her immediate family. For the most part, she has kept her pain to herself. She admits, however, that thoughts of suicide are never far away.

Jesse is, you might say, a poor historian. Her story is biased. She reports the negative experiences without giving so much as a glimpse at the positives in her life. She summarizes her life with her oft repeated line, "I always mess things up." Her existence, it would seem, is made up of one failure after another. When I challenge her facts and suggest that there have been triumphs, she responds with, "You don't understand." And this is how the game is played. I point her toward the positive aspects of herself and she tells me, "You don't understand." What she is trying to tell me, of course, is "If you really understood me, you would know there is nothing good about me."

Jesse tries hard to control our sessions. She worries that if she gives up control, she might learn more terrible news about herself. She's sure she is filled with awfulness. But she only shares enough of this awfulness to keep people at a distance. The rest must remain hidden. She criticizes herself constantly. In the months we have been working together, she has tried to convince me how truly inadequate she is. At first, I tried to convince her otherwise. Seeing little progress with this approach, I switched gears. Instead, I began listening to her story without trying to make corrections. Many therapists don't like to do this and for good reason. It's hard to listen to someone you care about berate themselves. But sometimes people have to hold the pain before they can let it go.

For a while, Jesse's condition deteriorated. She, like many other people like her, thought that getting better would be too painful to bear. She became suicidal for a time. In the process of healing from shame, you see, you may get worse before you get better. Doors must be unlocked and secrets revealed. Ironically, though, when all those aspects of yourself that you thought were so terrible are finally exposed, then your strengths and blessings become illuminated as well. When you feel safe enough to share the worst of you, you are probably in a place healthy enough to bring out the best in you.

Jesse is now beginning to tell her real story. Occasionally she falls back into the "I always mess things up" pathology. But these relapses are now fewer and farther between. She has managed to reveal more of herself than she had previously thought possible. And the sky hasn't fallen, the world hasn't ended, and she has not been abandoned. I'm not sure where she will go from this point. This will be up to her. I do know that she is freer, stronger, and more confident. She is coming to realize that she is good enough to have a good life.

There is also a second step to this stage that often gets missed. Besides telling your own story, it can help to listen to others as they share their personal histories. People with low self-esteem tend to overestimate the good fortune of others. They see themselves at the bottom of the pile with everyone above them. They don't always recognize that others carry their own crosses. Listening to friends, family, or fellow members of a support group explain what their lives have been builds a sense of connectedness. A connectedness that is often missing in those who feel inferior. They learn that we have all had to face discouragement. They see that we have all had fears and doubts about ourselves. Once you hear someone else give an honest personal history, you are less likely to feel inferior to that courageous soul. Nor will you feel superior. When healthy, honest relationships develop, no one has a need for superiority or inferiority.

Genuinely listening to other human beings can do much to relieve shame. Shame is about isolation. Listening helps dissolve isolation. The eminent psychologist Carl Rogers used to say that feeling understood is very similar to the feeling of being loved. Learning to love sometimes begins by learning to understand people (including ourselves). When you tell your story, you must listen carefully to it. When you listen to another person's story, allow yourself to feel it. No two people have identical stories. And there is no one with a completely unique tale. We all have so many things in common. You will hear parts of your story in everyone else's. And they will hear pieces of their story in yours.

Own It

Your story must lead to the present. If it remains stuck in the past, then it is not a living, vibrant, or accurate account of your life. People who feel inadequate are frequently enmeshed with the past. They are caught in the hurts and humiliations that keep them from entering the now. Among the casualties of this bondage is the ability to forgive. Forgiveness involves moving on and getting on with your life. You can't move on if you won't let go (at least a little) of the past.

You must tend to the present. If you don't, your past will define you. While our experiences certainly have an impact on who we are, they should not have the only word. By living in the present, we take control of what we will do with our experiences, how we will interpret them, how we will heal the wounds. One of the clearest indicators that we are controlled by the past is the use of blaming. People who constantly blame others for the crosses they bear are people who refuse to take responsibility for their lives. They tend to see themselves as victims, martyrs, sacrificial lambs, or scapegoats. They are re-luctant to see that they have choices in the here and now that will directly influence their lives. Living in the present empowers you to build yourself.

You may be able to identify people in your life who have harmed you. These individuals may have caused you to begin doubting yourself. They may have insisted that you were and would always be deficient. Their discouragement may have been overt or covert. Perhaps they were abusive or neglectful when you were most vulnerable or when you needed them most. Maybe the mistakes they made were well intended or perhaps they were intentionally cruel. You may have con-tributed to the problem or you may have been a completely innocent victim. You don't have to deny pain or minimize cruelty or overlook insensitivity and inconsideration in order to rise above the past. You can be honest and aware of a difficult past and choose to become healthy in the here and now.

Someone else may well be the cause of your shame, but you are responsible for continuing it. Perhaps you fell short of a powerful person's expectations. But now *you* are a powerful person, and you decide your own goals. You decide if you will distort yourself in order to become what your parents wanted. You decide whether the person who couldn't make friends as a teenager can become happy, confident, and successful. No matter how you have been trained by the people and experiences in your life, you decide whether you will hold your head up and look people in the eye. You decide on the standards that measure your character. You decide whether or not to believe the lie that says you are inadequate.

If you feel poorly about yourself, you must admit this to yourself. Accept the fact without looking for someone to blame. Healthy people look for solutions to their problems. Unhealthy people usually just look for someone to blame. Accept the fact that you have been hiding. Accept the fact that you've spent too much of your life feeling unworthy. Take the here and now as a reality. Understand that this is not how your life has to be. You have a present and a future, and they can be quite different from your past. Accepting where you are now is a starting point. It remains to be seen what comes next.

When you tell your story, you must describe in detail where, who, and how you are now. Reveal yourself in the moment. Explain how you are unique. Describe the similarities you see between yourself and others. Illuminate your gifts. Courageously articulate the aspects of yourself that seem to be less than adequate. Refuse to lump those inadequacies into vague terms such as "Everything's wrong with me." This is a cop-out. It's just another way of saying, "I'm not going to look at myself." If you think everything is wrong with you, then you haven't been introduced to yourself. If you only know your faults, you don't know who you are. Your story must include an examination of both your positives and negatives.

You may recall that earlier in the book I suggested that it is terribly difficult to tolerate the awareness of shame. We cannot hold this thought for long. It is simply too painful. In mild to moderate cases of shame, we may be able to maintain this awareness to one degree or another. But when feelings of inadequacy move from moderate to severe, we fight to move the feelings out of our awareness. The pain is too intense. To relieve the suffering, we move in one of two directions. We will either try to reject the reality through denial, projection, repression, distraction, blaming, or any of a number of unhealthy defenses, or we can choose to heal this wound. In other words, once you honestly face your feelings of inadequacy, you will decide to move forward or backward. In the past, you may have opted to regress whenever you felt the pain of inferiority. But if you have allowed yourself hope, you are much more likely to begin healing. Hope is key. Awareness of shame without hope usually leads to regression, pathology, more secrets, more shame. When the awareness of shame exists alongside even a small amount of hope, however, healing begins, the secrets dwindle, and you become empowered to decide how you will judge yourself.

Feeling inadequate is uncomfortable. But in order to heal, you must face the shame and decide what you will do with it. These feelings are your feelings. They may have begun while you were quite powerless, but you are not powerless now. The standards you seek to achieve are self-imposed. You maintain that ideal that causes you to feel inferior. You have the power to destroy yourself. You do not, however, have to use your power that way. You could use your power to love yourself and gently push yourself to grow in the directions that are truly meaningful to you.

Recovery from shame often takes a giant step forward when you admit, "I have felt inadequate for some time." Remember, shame thrives in hiding, and anything that breaks the pattern of concealing yourself can be helpful (as long as this exposure occurs in a context that is caring and supportive). If you can acknowledge your feelings of inadequacy and still manage to accept yourself, healing has begun.

Then you must own these feelings. They are yours. Take responsibility for them. They may have been with you for what seems like forever, but they don't have to last through eternity. Take responsibility for these feelings. Hold them, and they will not be able to hold you. They may have started in your home or on the playground or in the classroom. Perhaps they were solidified in a painful adolescence. But now the insults are coming from within. At times, that inner voice may sound like someone else's, but, be assured, it is your voice. The events of your life have convinced you that you are not good enough. Your experiences have led you to believe the lie. At this very moment you may still believe the lie. Please understand that you cannot wait for apologies; they may never come. Although apologies would be nice, you don't need them. You don't need anyone's permission to transform yourself from a victim to a survivor.

Many people who live with inferiority spend their lives waiting for a particular person to love them. They conclude that they can't be whole until mother, father, childhood friend, teacher, coach, or all these people come to them and express unconditional love. Once more, this would be wonderful, but it might not happen. You might wait forever without them knocking at your door. You don't need them to become good enough. If they will not or cannot help you, you are going to have to help yourself. Since you are responsible for how you feel about yourself, you can begin by changing the tapes that play in your head. For example, if you are still caught in the grasp of shame, at least be honest about it. Understand that you are not good enough for you. You discourage yourself. No longer is anyone responsible for this but you. Even if you are not quite ready to heal, you are capable of being honest about what you are dealing with. Others may have taught you how to be ashamed of yourself, but you are running the show now.

Eventually, as healing unfolds, you will need to send yourself other new messages. You will need to send yourself messages of confidence such as, "I can improve myself! I can survive! I can be a good human being! I can be strong! I can rise above and beyond the past!" You have the voice of confidence inside you and, if you let it, it will inspire you. You will also need to send yourself messages that build humility, messages like: "I don't have to be perfect. I have flaws but I'm still okay. There are lessons in my mistakes. I will be as healthy as the messages I send myself."

As you tell your story and take responsibility for your choices, you begin to live a more honest life. You gradually do away with the secrets and the hiding. Shame, you will recall, is a lie. As honesty and openness increase, the lie begins to fade.

Forgiveness

You have an enormous capacity to heal the wounds that life inflicts upon you. You can heal because you possess the power to forgive. Forgiveness is a choice. You may have decided that you are incapable of forgiveness. This is one of the tragic choices shame makes for you. Once shame takes your power to forgive, it robs you of your power to heal. The truth is, you always have the power to forgive. It may take time, but the power is always there.

By the way, not only is forgiveness a part of healing; it is also a fundamental ingredient in love. Without forgiveness, imperfect human beings could not coexist. Martin Luther King said: "He who is devoid of the power to forgive is devoid of the power to love." This also applies to your feelings toward yourself. You will not love yourself until you learn to forgive yourself. Forgiveness allows you to let go of your mistakes and failures. If you cannot forgive yourself, these scars accumulate. As they do, you come to feel rather ugly.

Holding on to people who have shamed you can be equally crippling. Your shame may end when you let go of the people who have shamed you. Many people resist forgiving those

who have hurt them because they believe forgiveness requires them to reenter a relationship with the offender. This
is an unfortunate, although popular, misconception. Forgiveness simply means you choose to release the anger and hurt
connected with a particular individual. That's all. It does not
mean that you must deny or minimize what you have been
through. It does not mean that you have to reestablish a relationship with that person. Forgiveness means you let go of the
pain that binds you to the past. There is, you see, a difference
between forgiveness and reconciliation. If I forgive you, I let
go of the resentment I have toward you. I can do this without
permission, restitution, or an apology. If we are to achieve reconciliation, however, we will have to come together to work
to restore our relationship.

You may have encountered situations in life where you have
forgiven someone, yet have not moved toward reconciliation.
Perhaps the person who hurt you had not made the changes
needed to make this a healthy relationship. Forgiveness freed
you to move on with your life without the hurt and anger.
Because reconciliation was not possible, you may have had to
grieve the loss of a relationship that was once very important
to you.

There are several relevant points here. First, some people
believe that if they have not fully reconciled with the person
they believe hurt them, then they have not forgiven. This is
not necessarily true. There can be forgiveness without reconciliation. You have a great deal of control over whether or not
you will forgive (although you may not control how long it
takes). You do not have nearly as much control over whether
or not reconciliation will be possible. Reconciliation requires
that both parties work together. Because you cannot control
the behavior of others, you cannot force reconciliation with
another human being.

This leads to a second significant point. You may not want to restore your relationship with the person (or people) who hurt you. Some people, for instance, spend their lives trying to attain the approval of a parent. With each attempt comes another failure with their self-confidence deteriorating each time. If you are caught in this sinking ship, you may have to accept, at some point, that the relationship will never be the one you deserve. You will then need to accept the loss, grieve the loss, and move on. Moving on involves finding healthier ways to get your needs met. You may, for example, need to find others who will nurture, encourage, and support you. Forgiveness means letting go of shaming experiences. It should not mean putting yourself back in those arenas that led you to feel bad about yourself.

Also, when you forgive yourself for mistakes you have made, this does not mean you must return and become the person you were. You can forgive yourself and then move on to become a healthier person. Forgiving does not mean forgetting. It means accepting what was with a conviction not to make the same moves again. Forgiveness is not so much about reconnecting with the past. It's more about letting go of the hurts of the past and reconnecting with your present and future. Shame lives, largely, in the past. Often, when you move into the here and now with a solid sense of future, shame has nowhere to live.

We understand some of the significant dimensions of forgiveness. We know that forgiving people comes easier when we seek to understand them. The mile we walk in their shoes is often the road to forgiveness. We also know that allowing ourselves to feel our pain is, ultimately, beneficial. We must hold the pain before we can let it go. We know, too, that forgiveness has its own timetable. We can treat the wound intelligently, aggressively, and gently, yet forgiveness occurs in its own time. We can assist the healing process, but we cannot force it.

If you feel bad about yourself, you need to place more energy in hope and less energy in hurt. Forgiveness begins with a decision. You choose to forgive. The process begins in earnest when you make an honest decision to try to reduce the resentment you feel toward one who has hurt you. You need to name and explain the injury. As you tell your story, you must describe in detail the person (or people) who have hurt you. Detail the events. By bringing these events out into the open you take them out of hiding.

Small hurts may be forgotten, but the big ones will not. Forgive and forget may sound nice, but it won't likely happen. You can't simply choose to delete events from your history. You will have to forgive and remember. But if you can forgive, those memories will change. You will not be tied to them as you once were. They will not own as much of your energy or attention. You will still have the memories, but they will no longer have you. You empower your bad memories by refusing to speak them. Their power is in silence. Once you begin to speak them, you begin to own them.

In the twelve step programs such as Alcoholics Anonymous, they use the expression, "Name it. Claim it. And tame it." This advice has been used in a variety of situations, but it is particularly relevant to our discussion. In order to resolve past hurts, you must first name the wound. Explain how you were hurt and why it has pained you so much. If one certain hurt reminds you of other injuries, name them too. If, when you describe them all, you still feel there is more to say, stay with it. Don't stop until you've put the stories into words. For the big hurts, you will have to tell the story several, or many, times. You need to keep telling your story until you feel the energy move from the past into the future. When this occurs, you may find yourself paying more attention to the person, or people, you are speaking with. This means that more of your attention and energies are focused on the here and now. You will eventually find yourself tired of those unfortunate tales that once consumed you. But moving on will require that you name all the characters, feelings, and features of your hurts and resentments.

Once you name and reveal your demons, you must do something that can be extremely trying for people with low self-esteem. You need to "claim it." This means honestly and courageously placing responsibility where it belongs. This may be especially difficult, because your feelings of inadequacy have biased your perceptions. You take too much responsibility for your failures and not enough for your successes. You tend to prematurely conclude that bad experiences are your fault. You may attempt to tell yourself that everyone else is to blame, but deep inside, you're sure it's your fault. This sets the stage for the confusing and frustrating practice of trying to forgive yourself for wrongs you have not committed. You don't get anywhere, but you don't know why. You may have found yourself locked into the all too popular dance called, "I try to forgive myself, but I can't." You can't forgive yourself for someone else's crimes. And you can't successfully forgive others for your offenses.

You have to place blame where it belongs. You need to claim responsibility for that which you are responsible. You must then give responsibility to those who are also responsible for your wounds. In order to forgive, you need to correctly identify those who need to be forgiven. You may have contributed to your own pain. But you must look at your life bravely and truthfully to balance the scales of blame. "This is one reason that many people who were harmed in childhood do not forgive," writes author and therapist Beverly Flanigan.

"It takes maturation to blame someone else and thereby to identify who really must be forgiven."[13]

You may also, of course, be tempted to go to the other extreme, blaming others for everything unfortunate that has occurred in your life. But if you have, this has probably been an attempt to deceive people. Blaming them may also serve to keep them from getting too close. No matter what you show the world, inside you blame yourself. You blame yourself for all your difficulties. You may also blame yourself for everyone else's woes.

In order to achieve forgiveness, you must find the balance. Claim the responsibility that is rightfully yours. Maybe you did make poor decisions that led to the collapse of your marriage. Own this. But then place the rest of the blame where it belongs. Identify how your ex-spouse injured you. When the balance is struck, you may find you need both to forgive and to apologize. Granting forgiveness, like asking for forgiveness, requires strength. "Forgiving," Flanigan rightly observes, "comes from a position of strength, not weakness."[14] Forgiveness arises from strength and then builds strength. Forgiveness makes you stronger. Each time you forgive, you become more familiar with the process. Forgiveness begets forgiveness.

In many ways, shame can be likened to a monster—one that feeds on resentment and secrecy. But this monster can be tamed. In order to get out from under shame, you must release the people and experiences that live inside you and continue to shame you.

The Basics

Shame is painful. No one wants to feel this way. Even when you bury it so deep that you no longer recognize it, it still hurts. True, there are those who play the "woe is me" game, where they act deflated in order to get attention, sympathy, or some other reward. They play a role, a role they choose. They are the perpetual martyrs, the chronic manipulators who choose to wallow in self-pity as a means of obtaining power over others. They may appear to be shamed, but their appearance is their way of empowering themselves. Shame is not at all their biggest problem. Honesty is.

Genuine shame, however, is always painful. There are no rewards for staying this way. Your feelings of inadequacy may cause you to act in such a way that decreases the likelihood of more hurt, but it doesn't ease your suffering. Genuinely believing you are not good enough has absolutely no rewards. Shame is a lie, but that does not necessarily make you a liar. You have been misled. As long as you believe that you can never be good enough, you will always be correct. You will have no incentive to try if there is no hope. All the rules change, though, once hope emerges. The future opens up and you are no longer tyrannized by the past. Hope alone will not be enough to free you, but it creates a destination, a goal. This destination, once you start to build it, begins to motivate you to fight your way toward it. Hope is the thought that says, "Maybe I can get there. Maybe I can feel better about myself. Maybe I can be good enough."

At some point on this road to recovery, you will have to introduce the real you. You may have to start by introducing the real you to yourself. You can do this by journaling, writing your autobiography, or telling your story to a tape recorder. Eventually, however, you will have to allow the real you some human contact. You will have to share who you are with other human beings. Without this self-disclosure, you will be keeping the secrets that feed the monster. Sometimes it's easier to begin this contact with a letter and then move toward personal contact. It really doesn't matter how small the steps are, as long as you keep moving.

You can control your movement. You decide when to reveal yourself. You decide to reach out. You choose to forgive. You may not select the obstacles that cross your path, but it is your choice what you will do with those obstacles. You may not control the amount of time it takes to heal, but you do have the power to move to where you need to be. You cannot change the past, but you can change your attitude toward it. Accept the things you can control as well as the things you cannot. Above all, remember that you always have the power to make the next right move. You have the power to make your next decision a good one.

Remember, too, that shame is a destructive form of protection. When nothing else works, shame hides you with the promise that you will not be hurt again. When you begin to come out of hiding, feelings of shame are likely to reappear in an effort to pull you back into the shadows. In the early stages of recovery, your battle between health and sickness may intensify for a time. Many of my patients, for instance, report that in the early stages of their recovery, they experience an increase in humiliation dreams. They dream of themselves in situations where they are ridiculed or demoralized. As unsettling as these dreams may be, it is often on the stage of dreams where the conquest of inadequacy is most clearly seen. As people become healthier, they become stronger in their own dreams. The various forces that symbolize shame are gradually defeated, leaving the dreamer encouraged and empowered. The lesson: humiliation dreams can give way to dreams of triumph.

At this point in your recovery, you need to keep moving. Fear will arise. Walk through it. A woman in her early fifties who had worked through severe feelings of inferiority that she had carried most of her life summed this up perfectly: "When you're convinced you can't, you can't!" It's that simple. Refuse to allow anyone or anything to take your hope away. Reach out to people who can help you. Find a good doctor if you don't already have one, and get a good physical examination. See if there might be a physical condition that might be limiting your energy. If you are to keep moving toward a healthier you, you will need your energy. Every day reveal yourself a little more. Hope. Touch. Talk. Take and give responsibility. Forgive. These will keep you moving in the right direction.

Finally, know that the signs of recovery may not be what you think. Be aware of growth in unexpected places. Some people believe that feeling better about themselves means that they will become extroverted, talkative, funnier, more popular, or more likely to receive a promotion. Well, not necessarily. As you feel better about yourself, you will become more like the person you really are. You will become more aware of what is most important to you. You may find out that you are a bit quiet and something of an introvert. That's wonderful! Do it well and be happy!

As you become more accepting of yourself, you may find new interests. Life will reach out to you and invite you to live and learn. The referees will fade from your world. At one time it seemed as if everyone were judging you. But no more. And all those who you thought were superior to you, well, their imperfections start to become more apparent. People will become more real to you. You see them as they are—imperfect and very human. Gradually, the world will become friendlier. In time, fear will be replaced with gratitude.

But healing always seems to have unique twists. We all heal in our own special ways. Take Carla, for example. Carla had actually already begun to heal before she came to see me. Perhaps her greatest achievement in her conquest of shame came through her singing. She had a magnificent voice, but she could not bring herself to sing before an audience. This was far too much exposure and self-revelation. She couldn't tolerate it. As she came out from under her shame, she started to sing. She began to sing with a voice and a passion seldom heard. She now is a much sought after soloist specializing in religious music. Carla and her voice spent years hiding. Now they have emerged.

Chapter Four

More Healing

There is more. Rising above inadequacy involves some immediate moves and some lifestyle changes. We discussed some of the more immediate changes in the last chapter. Seeing the hope. Reaching out to others. Telling your story. Owning the pain. And finally, forgiveness. These decisions all bring you closer to accepting yourself. How long does it take to accomplish these goals? Well, you never really achieve them as much as you live them. They are changes you can make at any time, yet every day you decide whether or not you will continue living them.

Inadequacy can be what the philosophers call a fixed idea. It can be a thought that becomes "fixed" in one's mind so deeply that it is considered permanent. Once an idea becomes fixed, it may stay in place for the rest of one's life. If your sense of inferiority has become a fixed idea, then it may not lift easily. Change may come only as you live a life that will destroy this malignancy. You can't wait for your self-respect to improve before changing your life. You have to change some aspects of yourself to defeat the shame.

Pete, for example, had everything he needed to be successful except a belief in himself. He had been a star football player in high school and had been given an assortment of college scholarship offers. He turned them down because he didn't think he could make it in college. He spent his twenties and thirties working as a laborer in various settings. Eventually, he worked himself into a position where he could use his considerable carpentry skills, but he never rose above what he called "low man on the totem pole." All the while, he dug himself into the hole of alcoholism.

In his late thirties he found Alcoholics Anonymous and began to heal. He became a fervent member of the local AA community and, within this context, he found a way to tell his story to supportive souls. He helped others and worked hard to release his resentments. In particular, he wanted to let go of the anger he felt toward his father. His father had been, until he died, very critical of Pete. You might say that Pete's father taught Pete how to criticize himself. Father gave son a series of verbal assaults that took root in his psyche. "You're awful." "You'll never amount to anything." "You're not much of a son." And on and on.

Pete had six years of sobriety at the time that he came to see me. He had already done a lot of healing, but he couldn't get past the voices. He knew where and how they originated, but he couldn't put them to rest. In the course of our work together, several important events occurred. First, he received a physical examination. This is almost always a healthy move for those who have struggled to care for themselves. Second, it became clear that Pete's family had a significant history of depression. Consequently, his family physician started him on an antidepressant. More healing. Still, the voices of discouragement lingered.

Pete worked hard to reduce his smoking habit. But, just as he could not eliminate the discouraging voices in his head, he could not rid himself of the cigarettes. I began to wonder if he lit a cigarette every time he heard the critic in his head. At first, he said he wasn't aware of such a connection but that he would be willing to try an experiment I proposed. He used a silver flip-top lighter, the kind that used to be popular back in the 1960s. I had him get the lighter engraved with the statement: "It's a lie!" Whenever he was tormented by the critical voice within, he was to read his lighter.

Healing from shame is about a few big items and a lot of little things. A few years later I ran into Pete. We talked for a while and just before we ended, I asked him about the lighter. He gave me a huge smile and said, "You know, I'm not sure. I kept it for the longest time, even after I stopped smoking. I held on to it even after it broke." It was clear he didn't need it anymore. Pete went on to start his own business and now owns a successful construction company. Becoming good enough means becoming healthy. Healthy is a lifestyle. Just as shame is a lifestyle, so too is self-respect. In order to live the lifestyle of healthy self-respect, you need to develop and maintain healthy attitudes and behaviors. It also means being in touch with your feelings and accepting them as an authentic dimension of yourself. Above all, you will need to make good decisions—decisions that keep you healthy rather than shameful. The healthy lifestyle can be described in many ways. I will focus here on those elements that are most relevant to those brave souls who are determined to rise above inadequacy.

You may have relapses along the way. When these occur, you will be tempted to conclude that you're back at square one. Don't you believe it. To keep growing through the relapses, keep in mind the fundamental fact about shame: "It's a lie!"

Healing Attitudes

The philosopher Nietzsche wrote, "That which does not kill me makes me stronger." He knew that the crosses we carry can ultimately empower us. This is true of shame. If your sense of inferiority has not destroyed you, then your experience with this monster can strengthen you. The years you have spent wrestling with this beast may have indeed given you the strength to become everything you are meant to be.

You must move out of the role of victim. There may have been a time when you had no choice but to be a victim, but things have changed. It is no sin to be victimized, but it is a tragedy to live your life as a victim. You are not a victim. You are a survivor. You have survived the wounds life has inflicted upon you, and you have survived the abuse you have inflicted upon yourself. It is not enough to know this; you must live it. Recognizing yourself as a survivor is more than an idea. It is an attitude. Survivors look and sound different from victims. Survivors walk with their heads up and look people in the eye. Your bad memories are not evidence of powerlessness; rather, they are descriptions of the hardships you have conquered. As you come to know yourself as a survivor, you feel empowered and walk stronger. Learning to walk strong may be a lot like learning to walk all over again. You take it one step at a time, and for a while you may fall a lot. But because you are a survivor, you have the ability to right yourself. Gradually, your strength builds until you lose the fear of falling.

You learn to walk strong one step at a time. The more you practice, the better you get. Try to put quiet power in your steps. Keep your head up. Survivors are people who keep going even when they tell themselves they have given up. Some gift inside keeps them moving. Unfortunately, too many people never see this gift in themselves. If you can recognize your talent as a survivor, you become stronger. Awareness of the strength that already exists leads to further empowerment.

A funny thing happens as this empowerment builds. You

will feel your sense of gratitude deepening. A survivor is not defeated by the dark side of life. Survivors are aware that this darkness exists, but they never become a part of that darkness. As the darkness tries to hold them down, survivors keep walking. It might seem that everyone who is a survivor would be grateful for that survival, but this isn't always the case. When gratitude begins inside you, it will not be for anything about you. What I mean is, if you were grateful for what you are, you wouldn't feel inadequate. You have always resisted being grateful for your life. It's never felt right.

This lack of gratitude has cost you. Gratitude contributes to happiness. Gratitude helps decrease anxiety, depression, and hostility. It lifts one's energy as well as one's generosity. Grateful people are giving people. Gratitude also has a special power to join people. It is much harder to feel inferior when you allow yourself to be grateful. But as I said, you have always resisted being grateful for the person you are. The fact is, when you become grateful for who you are, you will no longer need a book like this.

You will most likely begin to grow gratitude by focusing on external gifts—things like food, shelter, medicine, nice weather. I highly recommend that you write your own gratitude list. Start by writing a list of, say, fifty items. If that sounds like too many, look at your world a little more carefully. Go through your day. If you wake in a bed, then there is item No. 1. Be grateful you have a bed. Then consider being grateful for your toothbrush, shoes, clothes, and cereal. Having the car start or the bus arrive might give you cause for thanks. Now if you are saying to yourself, "These things don't count," think about what life would be without them. Keep this list near you. It may be crucial to your healing. Once survivors start growing gratitude, miraculous events seem to occur. Personal growth starts to take off.

Once you have learned to keep a gratitude list that focuses on the externals, you must then look at yourself for reasons to be grateful. You may be tempted to stop this exercise before it begins with an automatic thought such as, "There is nothing here to be thankful for." So, again, start at the beginning. If you can read, you have something about yourself to be grateful for. If you have been a survivor, this is another wonderful trait to be thankful for. In the early stages of your healing, you may still not like yourself. It is, however, crucial that you do everything within your power to be *fair* with yourself. List your faults if you feel you need to, but then compose what may be the more difficult list of your gifts. Begin with the basics (for example, I can read, I can think, I can laugh, ...) and work your way up to the hidden gifts (for example, I can change my life).

As you start to see your gifts, you must keep them in mind until you *feel* them. The gratitude attitude produces a feeling, a healthy positive feeling that makes life worth living. Your healing is in the feeling. You begin by growing gratitude for all your external gifts. Next you start to feel thankful for pieces of yourself. With each piece that leads to gratitude, you become a little freer from the shame you have carried.

Sometimes developing gratitude becomes easier if you build another attitude, one that says, "I will appreciate beauty." Only you can decide what strikes you as beautiful. Your sense of humor may be beautiful. Your sensitivity may be awesome. Your gift for feeling so deeply may be marvelous. Your spirituality may be truly wonderful. People who feel shame are often people who have let others define beauty for them. Caitlin, for example, has a gorgeous sense of humor. But she doesn't see it that way. She doesn't really share her humor. Instead, it slips out from time to time. It seems she can make people laugh at will but she is stingy with her talent. She keeps it under wraps. She doesn't see her humor as much of a gift and consequently there is no cause for gratitude.

If Caitlin is to heal, we can predict that several things will need to occur. She will need to recognize her gifts. Even if no one ever described her humor as beautiful, she will need to see its beauty. Once she recognizes this beautiful gift, she will need to allow herself to feel grateful for it. Feeling grateful for something about herself will be essential if she is to feel better about herself. Finally, she will need to allow herself the spontaneity needed to have this gift blossom. It has been hidden far too long. She, like many people who feel inadequate, will begin to reveal herself one piece at a time. Often the process looks like this:

Recognition → Gratitude → Revelation.

It is too soon to know what will happen with Caitlin. In a recent session, I told her that as she gets healthier she will become funnier. Just as I suspected, upon hearing this she fought to keep a smile from spreading across her face. She has been fighting a force (that is, her humor) that has been trying to surface. I think she is beginning to recognize its beauty. Hopefully, she will come to be grateful for it. If so, she may decide to share more of herself through her gift of humor.

Finding your beauty can be a challenge. It is hard to see your own strength when it feels like everyone else is looking at your flaws. This is especially true for those who have physical qualities that are described as abnormal. If your height, weight, or facial features don't fit the mold "normal," it may be even more difficult to find your beauty. So many people build their identities around their imperfections (or what they believe are imperfections). If you have built your identity around your weaknesses, you will feel weak. Even when everyone else seems to be staring at your flaws, you must keep a balance. Be aware of your shortcomings and then look for your beauty. It's there. When you find your beauty, you may even be empowered enough to feel grateful.

Shame is about keeping secrets. You are probably aware of this by now. But you might not be aware that among the secrets you have kept are your talents. When you started keeping secrets you were in control of the process. After a while it became automatic. Then it became out of control. Then *you* became a secret. In order to see your gifts, you must develop another new attitude: no secrets. Certainly you are entitled to your privacy, but you are prone to use "privacy" as a way to rationalize your unhealthy secret keeping. In the last chapter, we discussed telling your story, and this clears out all the old accumulated secrets that have been dragging you down. But now you must add the no secret attitude to your lifestyle so you don't begin a new collection.

Someone who is intent upon keeping secrets can find just as many reasons to continue keeping secrets as the gossip has for gossiping. There is a time for privacy and a time for discretion, but you must know that secrecy can destroy you. When you keep too many secrets, you become a secret. When you become a secret (by hiding your real self), you are living in shame. If, however, you refuse to let yourself become one big secret, it is unlikely that your self-esteem will ever again drop to dangerous levels. Another sign that you are opening up and accepting more and more of yourself is the act of laughing at yourself. As you strengthen your resolve to look for humor in yourself, you will become stronger, more humble, and more human. If you can't find anything funny about yourself, keep looking. It's there. We all have quirks and absurdities. The freedom to laugh lovingly at yourself adds immense enjoyment to your life. It communicates a willingness to be human. It states clearly that you accept that you are not the best at everything. Honesty and gentleness are the key here. You can pretend to laugh at yourself when, in fact, you are not close to self-acceptance. You may even ridicule yourself with caustic humor that does little more than degrade yourself further. But with practice and determination, you can learn to laugh gently at yourself. Look for others who do this well and learn from them. Learn to laugh lovingly at yourself. The actress Ethel Barrymore once remarked, "You grow up the day you have your first real laugh—at yourself." As you begin to rise above your inadequacy, you start to see humor in places where you only saw pain. You might also get a few grins from places inside you where you were afraid to look. As you come to accept that even the strongest person has weaknesses, your weaknesses are less likely to make you feel inferior. Life gets a little easier if you can smile when you think about your struggles with math, your mechanical ineptness, your unusual voice, your awkwardness with the opposite sex, your fear of heights, or your skinny legs. I'm not suggesting that you laugh at all your hardships. I agree with Mark Twain who said, "You show me someone who knows what is funny and I'll show you someone who knows what is not." Someone with a good sense of humor knows what is and what is not funny. Not everything about your life is humorous. Your life is like one of those "find the hidden picture" puzzles. There is humor hidden all over the place. When you find the humor, you feel healthier.

Feelings

Shame is, as much as anything, a feeling, a painful feeling. Given time and room to grow, it can become one's only feeling. It can take up so much space and energy within that all other emotions are banished into the darkness. In order to be really happy, all your feelings must have a voice, and they must be given freedom of speech. You have to allow yourself to feel. This may seem like curious advice because you may believe you already feel too much. Perhaps you would like to stop feeling altogether. This is understandable. If you have lived with shame long enough, it may seem like there are no good feelings.

You may also fear emotions because of their potential force. You may fear your own anger, for instance, for the damage it will do if you let it out. Or you think if you start to cry, you might cry forever. Or maybe one little scream will turn into all-out lunacy. You don't trust or value your feelings because they have always been an essential part of you. If you are inadequate, your feelings must be inadequate or defective or dangerous. It is hard to fathom that you are filled with wonderful feelings that are waiting for the invitation to help make your life worth living.

You already know there are painful feelings. This will always be the case. Healthy feelings don't always tickle. You may have memories that will always cause heartache. Understand that in a full life there will be heartache. Everyone has painful experiences. Some pretend they don't. Some pretend so well that they fool themselves. But everyone knows hurt. Pain does not make you inferior; it makes you human.

But enough about pain. You're an expert on that subject, so we will move on. The most important feeling you need to nurture is love. Love is the stain remover that lifts shame. Shame has done everything it can to take love from your life, but love is an amazingly resilient force. It can be beaten and buried and still survive. It is hard to love while you feel so inadequate, but it is just as difficult to feel shame while you feel love. You may have to start small yet defiantly. Although it may feel as if an invisible authority figure is punishing you for it, begin by loving the small things. Things like your guitar, your bike, or your plants. Love a nice day or a great movie. Stop being so neutral or critical. Add more positive power. It is okay to love a great tasting apple or an awesome touchdown run. Loving the little things in life means you are on your way to loving your life.

You might be saying, "It's not that easy." But in fact, it is not that hard. Shame is a lie. It has told you that love is impossible. It has insisted that you can't love right and that no one can possibly love you. By this point in your life, the lie may have become so convincing that the idea of loving anything may seem close to hopeless. But remember, it is all a lie. You are as capable of loving as anyone. Shame may have critically wounded your confidence, but it cannot destroy your heart. Start where you are. Practice loving the small joys of life. Begin by really looking for them. Finding the small joys of life can be like finding the stars at night. When you first look at the night sky, you may not see a single star, but then after a little while, you find one. Once you see the first one, another appears and then another. Soon you see so many stars you can't imagine how there was ever a time when you missed them all.

Begin by loving the little things. As this feels more and more natural, you will move toward a deeper love of human beings. You will then move toward a love of life itself. During this time, your spirituality may take on a power it never has. Love takes you beyond yourself. That relentless self-consciousness that has plagued you vanishes when you feel love for someone or something. You cannot love and dwell on yourself at the same time. When shame crippled your willingness to love, you began to stare at yourself in a critical, punishing way. As you begin to empower your love, you will look toward life and others in a caring, affirming manner.

Love expresses itself in many ways. One way is through curiosity. When you love someone, you want to learn about that person. You want to hear that person's story. As you build a love for life, you become interested in more dimensions of your world. When you are ashamed of yourself, you are ashamed of your questions. Your questions are far too revealing to be allowed. Your questions are as unique as your fingerprints. They say so much about you. One of the best avenues to self-discovery is to simply follow your questions. Start small if you have to. The little questions can sneak past the censorship of shame and then eventually break the dike entirely. Then all your questions will be allowed expression.

I like the Zen aphorism that says, "When the mind is ready, a teacher appears." When you free your curiosity, teachers and learning experiences begin to spring up everywhere. An empowered curiosity will lead you to them. Your questions must be sincere. You may have asked yourself countless times, "Why do I feel this way about myself?" But you never actually looked for an answer. Follow the questions that are meaningful to you. Don't just ask them; strive to find answers. A free curiosity will keep you growing. As you learn, you grow, and an active curiosity can help keep you balanced. Given room to roam, your questions will focus on your internal world and then move beyond your self-consciousness to engage the world around you. You may continue to wonder, "Why do I get down on myself?" but with a liberated curiosity you may find yourself also asking, "How do computers work?" or "What would it be like to learn a foreign language?" or "How do gardens grow?" The world opens up before you. When you liberate your curiosity, you go a long way toward freeing yourself.

Follow your questions. Even the painful ones. You may well need to make sense of the years you have spent criticizing yourself. To forgive yourself, you will need to understand yourself and your experiences. To do so, you must point your curiosity toward the past and the present, looking both inside yourself and in all directions around you. With experience, your curiosity will grow wiser. You will learn that some questions lead nowhere. You may have spent years on the "What's wrong with me?" question without finding an answer. Some questions just don't help. When you get stuck on a question, listen for new ones. It may be, for instance, that what you really need is to ask yourself, "What's right about me?" You may be at a point where you can learn a lot more by examining your strengths.

Your curiosity is not perfect, but it is honest. If you trust it, it will lead you in healthy directions. If, however, it is controlled by shame, it will probably lead you to more shame.

Your feelings about yourself have also made it difficult for you to express fear and hurt. These are not emotions that empower you. They seem weak and you don't want to show weakness if you can possibly help it. You may have hidden your fear and hurt behind anger, bitterness, or a make-believe exterior that tries to convince others that "everything is just wonderful." But until you share your anxieties and sorrows, you will remain isolated. This may seem absurd. You may be saying something like, "That's all I do. I tell everyone I know how bad I feel." Well, take a good hard look at this. You may have been communicating all your reasons for staying stuck. Your disclosures of "honest emotion" may have been your way of explaining why you couldn't possibly grow into a happy, healthy, confident human being. All along, you may have been stating your case for remaining inadequate. All the while you have avoided acknowledging your true fears. You have concealed your fears of maturing into the person you really are.

Until you free yourself to share the fears and sorrows that matter most, you will remain isolated. Honest self-disclosure creates the ties that connect people. Without this connection, you are alone with the critical voices that have been in residence in your head. Good human relationships take you away from that hyper-reflection. To create the relationships you need, you must share some of the feelings that you have kept to yourself.

Besides the fear and hurt, another feeling that you must acknowledge is sadness. This too might sound strange. You may be quick to suggest that you have always felt the sadness. Maybe. But maybe not. Many people who feel inadequate are so focused on their critical voices that they never allow themselves to feel their own sadness. They may know it is there. They just never let themselves experience it. If you avoid your sadness, you will never be authentic. Authentic souls will allow themselves to feel what they feel. You may have convinced yourself that you could not tolerate your own sadness. But becoming aware of your sadness is another sign of your growing freedom. It's one of those paradoxes of the human condition; you become happier and healthier when you choose to feel all your emotions, even the sadness. When you make statements to yourself such as, "I can be sad," you loosen shame's grip. Sadness makes you human, not inferior.

Allow yourself to feel quietly. Allow yourself to feel out loud. It is not enough to do it just today or tomorrow. Being honest about your feelings must become a lifestyle. Shame loves to wait out new self-help strategies. Temporary solutions are just that, temporary. Permanent solutions require lifestyle changes. It is not enough to get in touch with your feelings for a few days. You need to live graciously with your emotions.

Behaviors

To use a popular cliché of the 1990s, "You can't just talk the talk. You have to walk the walk." Walking the walk is a behavior. Something that you do that can be seen by those around you. Many of the lifestyle changes you need to make begin on the inside. Your awareness of your feelings and the changes you make in your attitudes all begin within you. As your emotions and beliefs become healthier, they emerge and become more visible. As they do, you emerge and become stronger and more honest. The real you that has been hidden for so long starts to engage people. People start to say, "You've changed," and you have. As the real you emerges, the world sees a new and healthier you.

As you become more confident, you walk with your head a little higher and you spend more time looking folks in the eye. You don't present yourself as a pathetic bag of dark secrets. Instead, you encounter others as the flawed yet wonderful human being you are. You want people to like you, but you realize that you will not disintegrate if they don't. You are a survivor. You can be bloodied, but you need not be defeated.

You must become a contributor. Look to make your contributions. Make a donation. Give directions. Write that letter to the editor. Help push someone's car out of the snow. Recycle. Give blood. Keep contributing. Eventually, you will come to count yourself among the contributors (i.e., those naturally inclined to give of themselves for the greater good). It is not enough to do this for a week or two. If you want to feel good about who you are and what you have to offer, you must see and feel your contributions. Your life must be a statement to the world that you have gifts to share and you are willing to share them.

Your contributions are crucial to your healing, because,

through your contributions, you become a contributor, someone who has something worthwhile to give and is willing to
give it. But I would be guilty of exaggeration if I suggested that
contributors are immune to feelings of inferiority. Indeed, a
number of extremely talented and generous people have been
saddled with serious doubts about themselves. Barbara, for instance, is a tremendously talented educator who has received
a variety of awards for her selfless work with young people.
Now in her forties, she is for the first time becoming a friend to
herself. Looking back on her life, she now has answers to questions that have haunted her for years. More than anything,
perhaps, she couldn't comprehend why people wanted to be
near her. She saw people fighting to get into her classes but
she didn't understand why. She recently told me, "I couldn't
understand why people were wasting their time with me."

All of Barbara's contributions were not enough to bring her
to self-acceptance. It wasn't until she slowed her life down to
work on herself that she began to achieve an appreciation of
the person she is. She had some work to do on contributing
to herself. She also needed to discipline herself to really listen
to the gratitude she received. But we were helped by the fact
that Barbara was already a contributor. This crucial part of
recovery was already in place. She had all the skills required to
make each day productive and meaningful. She began to end
her days with the knowledge that: "today I made a difference."

No one skill is enough to turn self-condemnation into
self-respect. You build a healthier lifestyle one piece at a
time. Another important behavior to practice is affirmation.
Affirmation is the art of recognizing gifts and expressing appreciation for those blessings. Affirmation is an expression of
gratitude. It is a statement that says, "I recognize you. I value
you. I am grateful for you." Fundamental to affirmation is sin-
cerity. Flattery is manipulation. You can affirm someone only

when you realize and value that person's gifts. You can begin by developing an eye for people's strengths. Look for qualities in people that you value. This may take work because you tend to be too self-absorbed to really see other people, or because your jealousy has kept you from appreciating a talent someone else has that you lack. Affirming others, however, is a necessary part of a healthy lifestyle. An affirmation is your declaration that there is beauty and goodness in the world and that you are grateful for the positives in your life. Affirming others builds healthy relationships. Relationships grow as we continue to value each other. Affirmation is the expression of that appreciation.

As you grow in the art of affirmation, you will gradually become prepared for the advanced course—self-affirmation. Self-affirmation is in some ways your ultimate challenge. The process is similar to interpersonal affirmation. First, you recognize the gift or talent in someone. Second, you become aware that you sincerely value that quality. Finally, you express gratitude for that special ability. In self-affirmation you recognize the gift in you, you accept that it is indeed a special blessing, and you make an expression of gratitude for that which you have been given. This may be a considerable feat for you. Your first impulse may be to rationalize away this suggestion with an explanation such as, "It is vain to affirm yourself," or "Only a narcissist would seek to affirm herself," or the old tapes in your head might click on with, "There is nothing in me to affirm anyway."

If you can read these words, you have grounds for affirming yourself. The ability to read is one of the most marvelous skills you could ever develop. If you can see the print clearly with or without glasses, you have the gift of sight. It is hard to imagine many blessings more wonderful than this. But you have not given yourself credit for skills such as these because "everybody else can do these things." You have been caught in the trap of chronic comparison. You tell yourself, "Everyone can read," and "Everyone can see." Although, of course, this is not true, it usually seems that way to you. Your gifts, you have insisted, are nothing special. They don't lead to favorable comparison. You have grouped people into two categories: superior and inferior. Because you have placed yourself in the latter group, you have never expected to find much in yourself worth affirming. Sincere self-affirmation breaks this old, sick pattern. It does not involve comparison. It is simply about recognizing a gift, valuing that talent, and expressing gratitude for what you have been given. If everyone else who has ever lived has had the same advantage, fine. Be aware and grateful that you have it, too.

There will be times when the only affirmation available is self-affirmation. You may not always be surrounded by people willing to affirm. Knowing that you are able and willing to affirm yourself provides motivation from within—motivation that does not depend on the behavior of others. This is a trait of high achievers. They have the ability to motivate themselves. They carry an encouraging voice within them. Because it is a part of them, it is always with them. As you get better and better at affirming yourself, you build a powerful motivating force that can move you to accomplish more than you may have ever thought possible. As you practice the art of self-affirmation and your internal motivation grows, you will develop another behavior that assists your healing. You will begin to *emerge*. When you emerge, you come into yourself. You allow, even encourage, your uniqueness to present itself. You follow your own calling. Walk your true path. Build your special dreams. As you emerge, you leave your hiding place. You introduce yourself to yourself and to others. Your real self comes out of the dungeon.

Kelly, a former patient of mine, described this point in recovery well. Looking back on her life she told me, "I always thought that if the spotlight hit me, I would burn to death." She came to understand that emerging would not destroy her. She learned that exposure did not mean self-destruction. Her life then blossomed in many ways. She came out of hiding and emerged as a beautiful person.

I have been fortunate enough to have seen many people like Kelly emerge from the shadows and become the special people they are meant to be. I'm also quite aware that there are many others who spend their lives submerged in debilitating shame. At times I wonder just how many of us spend our lives hiding ourselves. My stomach tightens when I consider that Erich Fromm may have been right when he spoke of the tragedy that most of us die before we have begun to live.

Living your life to the fullest means expressing your real self. To do so, you must be willing to emerge from the crowd. If the spotlight hits you, it will not kill you. You can raise your hand and ask your question. You can stand and make your voice heard. You can be loved, and you can take your turn to be "the strong one" in your relationships. You have the courage and humility to apologize, but your life is not an endless string of apologies. You can affirm and self-affirm. You are able to keep your head up and look people in the eye. You feel gratitude and are able to express it clearly and often. You will always remember what it was like to feel inferior, but these memories do not have the power to own you or destroy you unless you let them. You have everything you need to make the world a better place. You may also find that the more you learn, the more good you can do.

Rising above inadequacy means changing your lifestyle. A healthy lifestyle includes efforts to care for your physical wellbeing. Physical exercise can be tremendously helpful. But you must find the workout that is right for you. Try different approaches. Walking, biking, aerobics, weight training, swimming, tennis—all have value. If your fitness routine is all work and no fun, it is doubtful you will stay with it. You need to find a fitness program that gets results and is enjoyable enough to keep you motivated. Some people pick a single workout, for example, swimming, and stay with it. Others mix and match, for example, tennis and walking. There is no single workout that is perfect for everyone. You need to tend to your physical health, but you must do so in a way that is right for you.

It is also important that you learn to relax. It is hard to be at peace with yourself if you cannot find peace. Sometimes a good fitness program can help you relax. But you may need more. Meditation can be helpful. Many people, of course, find religious practices to be quite helpful here as well.

Finally, there is courtesy. Do your best to treat people well. Be courteous to others and yourself. Maintain this balance. Develop good habits. This is a small but important part of recovery. Many people who feel completely incompetent are more than polite to others. They are so for several reasons. First, they are usually approval seekers, and manners help them gain approval. Second, they fear criticism and will do just about anything to avoid that. Third, they are genuinely good people who want the best for the people they touch.

As you move out of shame, your need for approval and your fear of criticism lose their strength. Now your biggest incentive to be good is the belief that it is the right thing to do. If you decide to work toward being a polite person, it will no longer be out of fear. Now it will be fueled by caring and love. Your kindnesses may have at one time been manifestations, and reminders, of your fears. Now they are reminders of your decency. You become a caring person by acting in caring ways, for the right reasons.

Decision Making

Your sense of inadequacy has impacted your life in many ways. It has influenced how you think, act, and feel. But its real power derives from its ability to affect your decision making. Your feelings of inferiority can spread and gain new ground in your system; they are always looking to make that big conquest, that one strategic assault that, if successful, will put shame in control of your life. This is the fight to gain control of your decision making. Once shame has taken this function, it controls the throne. It can now lead you to act in ways that generate greater and greater amounts of self-condemnation. It can lead you away from the people and experiences that might help you become healthy again. Moreover, it can lead you to self-destruction. The battle to control your decision making is monumental. You cannot live a happy, healthy life with shame making your choices. As long as this destructive force is deciding your moves, it will only make choices that keep it in power. It will make the decisions that bring more shame into your life.

In order to heal—and stay healthy—you must take control of your own decision making. You cannot let shame make your decisions. Regaining control begins with awareness. Even if your feelings of inferiority have long ago taken complete control of all your choices, you may not be aware of it. You may have lost control so gradually and over such a long period of time that the change may have been imperceptible. You may have thought all along that you have been trying to make good, healthy choices, when in fact your intentions have been quite the opposite. In truth, you may have been making decisions with the purpose of tearing yourself down. Understand that shame must not be allowed to make your selections in life. Ask yourself if this has been happening to you. Consider the possibility. When you make career plans,

is shame pointing you in a particular direction? How about
your choice of friends? Are your feelings of inferiority selecting your company? Is how you treat yourself and how you
treat others determined by your self-doubt? What about the
clothes you wear or how well you take care of your health?
Are these decisions made by shame?

After you have become aware that shame may indeed be
making some or all of your decisions, you will need to regain
control of your decision making process. Begin by using your
conscience. Look for the decisions you believe are right. Let
your feelings guide you, but don't let them choose your path
without consulting your intellect. Think through your moves
before you make them. Consider the consequences as far as
they may go. Be careful of quick decisions, particularly if you
have a history of making shameful choices. Focus your conscience, your intellect, and your emotions to make the best
possible decisions. Before you make your choices, ask yourself
if shame is pushing you in a particular direction. You may not
want to go where shame points you.

When you face a decision, try to determine all your options. Once you have determined your choices, consider using
the following incomplete sentences to point you in a healthy
direction. Look at your options and complete the following
sentences:

> The right thing to do is . . .
>
> The real me would . . .
>
> If I had more confidence, I would . . .
>
> I would feel good about myself if I . . .

These statements can help lead you to the choices that are
right for you. Choices that are right for your true self, not

the false self that may have been in power for a long time. Making healthy choices is a key aspect of a healthy lifestyle. It must be an ongoing effort. Shame can creep into anyone's life and there will never be a time when you are completely immune to it. The best defense is a healthy lifestyle. Part of a healthy lifestyle is remaining aware that shame may try again to control your decisions. Stay true to yourself. Follow your conscience. Use your intellect. Feel your feelings. Name the feelings that are influencing you. Decide which feelings will guide you. Refuse to allow shame to make your decisions for you.

Please Keep in Mind...

"I still visit Shame City," David told me, "but I used to live there." This simple statement tells us a lot about the recovery process. It came after David had worked hard to deal with severe shame issues. At the point he made this remark about his relationship with "Shame City," David had freed himself from the overpowering sense of inadequacy that had once owned him. But he had also come to accept that relapses happen. As he came to accept this, the relapses became fewer and less intense. He also realized that a bout with shame did not mean he had fallen back to the starting point. Rather, it meant he had to defeat the monster once more. Fortunately, he now had faith in his abilities to walk away from Shame City.

Relapses happen. Not because you are bad but because you are human. Anyone who feels will encounter self-doubts from time to time. Aging is a process of gaining and losing. Both may cause you to wonder if you are up to the challenges of your life. To an extent, your doubts help keep you grounded. They cause you to question and think, pause and ponder. Your doubts also help keep away grandiosity and arrogance, faults that affect so many of us.

Don't expect shame to leave your life completely. Healthy human beings are still prone to periods of self-condemnation. But shame need never control your life. It can only own you if you let it. There may be times when you find yourself visiting Shame City, but you don't have to live there.

If you are still unable to leave this awful place, you may want to enter counseling. If you are willing to take enough of a risk to be honest, a good counseling relationship may help pull you out of the quicksand. Asking for help is often the first significant step toward freedom. You may fear that therapy will only unearth more horrible dimensions of yourself that have evaded your consciousness. What is much more likely, however, is that a good therapeutic experience will introduce you to strengths that you never knew existed, gifts that were never allowed to reveal themselves while you were under the rule of the tyrant shame. Therapy is not about finding out how bad you are. It is about correcting the lie that has insisted you are not good enough.

Whether or not you opt for counseling, please remember: People who have been burdened and beaten by feelings of inferiority often conclude that they need to change everything about themselves. They look to reinvent themselves from the ground up. In a weird way this makes a certain amount of sense. If you believe you are inadequate, it may be logical to assume that you must turn yourself into someone who is good enough to be valued, respected, and loved. That "someone" may seem like a completely different person from who you are now. But this goal of total transformation is not only unnecessary; it is destructive. You can only change so much. Your personal history will remain essentially the same (although your attitudes toward it may change). Your genetic makeup will stay in place. In short, not everything about you can be altered. And trying to change dimensions of yourself that are essentially permanent will leave you frustrated. You will feel defeated because you will be trying to move a mountain that is not to be moved.

If you have lived with shame, you may be trying to change too much of yourself. You're not accustomed to believing this, but there is a great deal of you that is just fine. Indeed, there are qualities to you that are much more than fine. Keep these. Protect these. Honor these. You will be tempted to change too much. Refuse this temptation. Your first move will be to clear your vision. Look honestly at yourself and decide (without shame making the decision) what parts of you may need repair and what aspects deserve appreciation. You may find dimensions of yourself that you would like to repair but cannot. Accepting your imperfections may be quite a challenge for you, but it gets easier with practice. With a little concerted effort you can learn to smile and say, "So, I'm not perfect." As you get healthier you reach an important awakening. You learn that you don't have to be perfect to be valuable, respectable, and lovable. You can be flawed and more than good enough.

And as you come to see yourself as good enough, you may have another awakening. You may learn that you need to do some spiritual healing. All your questions about God and the meaning of your life are waiting to be answered. Feeling inadequate has caused you to fear revealing yourself. Perhaps even to your Higher Power. Indeed, the one you fear most may be the one who is most capable of seeing the real you. People have talked about being loved by God, but it may have been difficult for you to feel this. Feeling love has not been one of your strong points.

Maybe you have been shamed into believing what you have been told to believe. Or perhaps you have created a false self that appears to be quite religious. In either case, you have never really given yourself to the faith that you may profess. With your real self hidden away, you couldn't possibly.

Many people use their religion to help them find forgiveness. Again, this has been a chore for you. You may be able to rattle off a hundred sins you have committed starting around your second birthday, but there could be a select few transgressions that never get mentioned. One or two that are too terrible to reveal. They are classified as unforgivable and are far too atrocious to bring into a spiritual context. Beyond this, you have had trouble believing that you are worthy of forgiveness. There has been something special about you that makes you less forgivable than other people. You have thought, at least at times, that there is nothing in the spiritual world powerful enough to forgive you.

To really understand the power of shame, you must realize that it is capable of destroying one's image of God. It can make you perceive your Higher Power as a brutal, vindictive force that seeks to punish you for all the awful things you are. Or, because you have walled yourself off so thoroughly, there may be no feel to God. God may be little more than a story told in an attempt to make life more tolerable. Or you may have concluded that even if there is a loving God, you shouldn't let him get close enough to see the real you. So you see God off in the distance, a beautiful yet distant being. The lie that has told you that you could not possibly be good enough has kept you so alone.

Spiritual healing involves taking what you have learned and bringing it into your spiritual life. In many ways, this means opening a new set of doors. Sometimes it helps to follow your curiosity. Your questions can point you in the direction of what you need to know. These are some questions that might get you started. You will need, however, to listen to the questions that come from within you. What is your path in life? What do you hold sacred? How do you see God? How does God feel about you? If you have a faith, how will you live it? Do the opinions of others determine how you will live your spirituality? Are you ready to accept love? Do you have the courage to reveal yourself as one who values your spirituality?

Many treatments for shame will fall short because they never address the spiritual dimension. What often occurs in these situations is that even if people come to feel more confidence in themselves, they are left with the unsettling feeling that "something is still missing." Without tending to the spiritual, there is also the risk of becoming more confident, yet just as self-absorbed as when you were soaked in shame. To be truly healed from shame, you must come to realize that you are part of a grand universe. And whereas you once believed that you could not possibly be a significant contributor to this immense arena called life, you come to realize that not only are you able to make important contributions, you are also being called to do so.

Spiritual healing pulls you beyond egocentricity. Your focus shifts. You begin to look beyond yourself. That painful self-consciousness that tortured you becomes a fading memory. Your spiritual development must, of course, become part of your lifestyle.

Remember, the cure for shame is a healthy lifestyle. This lifestyle must include a conscious effort to develop your physical, psychological, and spiritual dimensions.

Chapter Five

Beyond Inadequacy

Those who have lived in shame and have risen above this wretched condition are among the most wonderful human beings one could ever meet. They are like worn, soft leather, unpretentious and vulnerable, strong and beautiful. As you shed your feelings of inadequacy, you free yourself to become a happy, healthy, and imperfect person living in a marvelously vibrant yet imperfect world. You will be humbled and empowered. You will be truly alive.

As shame loses its control over you, you evolve into a more courageous being. With the confidence that you can survive failure, you are willing to risk. You are willing to look for a new job, ask someone for a date, and write those poems that you have had inside you for so long. The world is not as frightening and thus you are willing to ride your curiosity wherever it may take you. As you come to love yourself, you learn to love your curiosity, your questions, and your drive to learn. As the love inside you is allowed expression, it multiplies. You are a person capable of loving, living in a world with so many things to love.

Without that sense of inferiority, you are free to reveal yourself to yourself and to the rest of the world. You are no longer filled with secrets. The lights are now on. Magnificent lights they are, too. While you are introducing yourself, you may find a dancer or a musician inside you. You may come across a leader or a master gardener or an insightful philosopher. Once shame leaves, you can begin the enlightening process of self-discovery. Everything about you that could have been can now be discovered. While you are discovering yourself, you become more supportive of others and less envious. You can laugh at yourself in a healthy way—a way that demonstrates your humility, insight, and self-acceptance. You no longer resent yourself or envy others because you have flaws. It's not the flaws that make you inadequate; it's what you believe about the flaws that have caused you to condemn yourself.

Without shame, you will find yourself on the threshold of a much deeper spirituality. Your spiritual needs are no longer signs of weakness. A Higher Power is not a crutch for defective souls. You will need time to develop this essential dimension, but as you allow yourself to be yourself, you will find this to be a very natural process. People who have felt healing in their lives are usually drawn to tend to their spirituality. I'll leave it to you to find out why.

Because you no longer project your hostile feelings onto others, the world becomes a safer, more tolerant, and accepting place. You are less tempted to live behind fortress walls. You still make mistakes, but now your mistakes are lessons. You are so much healthier because you learn from experience. Hurts still happen, but with each bruise life gives you, you take a lesson. Pain is no longer your conqueror; it is a teacher. Because you now have confidence in your ability to survive, you are not nearly as easily defeated. As you purge yourself of inner enemies, you become much more powerful and resilient. Without that self-contempt that has kept you prisoner for so long, you are no longer a desperate approval seeker. You are free to disagree, to have your own opinion, to speak your own thoughts and feelings in your own voice. You would prefer to get along with everyone, but you now understand that in a full life, there will be times when your contributions will not be appreciated and your views criticized. This criticism is no longer evidence of your inferiority; rather it is a testimony to your uniqueness. As you allow your real self to emerge, you will be writing a truly special life story.

One of the best indicators that you have freed yourself from shame is your ability to not only accept criticism, but on occasion to learn from it. Clearly, not all criticism is beneficial. Some will originate in another person's unresolved issues. Usually this is an attempt by that person to control you. If this tactic does not work, typically the criticism will stop. When you were convinced you were defective, criticism probably controlled you. As your shame leaves, the strategy loses its clout. You can hear criticism without crumbling. You may even reach a point where you can hear the fault finding, digest it, process it, and take from it information that can help you be a better person. In a way, you have the power to turn lead into gold. You can take the bitter and turn it into the sweet. You can now understand the adage, "Life is what you make of it."

You are more independent, yet your interpersonal relationships are growing deeper. There is now less risk of you losing yourself or giving yourself away in a relationship. You are constantly growing, so a certain amount of change is a constant in your life. You are willing to adjust for the sake of someone you care for. But you are not willing to change everything. You no longer need to. There may have been a time when you were willing to be anyone but who you really are, but those days are gone. There are dimensions of yourself that are too sacred to change. You may reexamine your conscience, for instance, but you are wise to be cautious about making changes here. You may want to strengthen your conscience. Compromising your sense of right and wrong for a relationship may be too much. Shakespeare gave sound advice when he wrote, "To thine own self be true." You will never be happy until you find a way to remain true to yourself.

As the self-loathing subsides, you lose the fear of what lives inside you. You no longer waste your energy repressing the real you. You allow yourself to be spontaneous and creative. No longer do you savagely scrutinize every thought that comes to mind or feeling that comes to heart. Your inner clown is given room to roam. Not every statement that comes out of your mouth is so well rehearsed that it sounds rote or phony. Instead, you revive the innocence and wonder that you once knew. This is authentic living. The real you is given the energy to thrive and the freedom to soar. Every day you encounter a world that is full of newness. Some of what you encounter is painful, but this does not blind you to the beauty. Every day you are reminded, too, of the newness that lives within you. Your real self is never boring. There is always something new there. Your real self is an adventurer and an explorer. You love the newness. Your added energy will not lead to perfection but it will empower you. There may be occasional visits to Shame City. Relapses, that is. The difference now is that when you feel shame, you are driven to overcome it. You make the changes needed to rise above those feelings of inadequacy. We all have times when we feel bad about ourselves. Being healthy does not mean completely avoiding these periods. Health involves recognizing these episodes for what they are and then making the changes needed to feel better about yourself. Sometimes, for instance, an honest apology can be the ticket out of Shame City.

Your self-doubts will become less frequent and less intense as you develop more and more experience walking away from shame. You are also less vulnerable to shame because you are

able to accept affirmation. You are stronger because you can
hear the good stuff. As shame loses its grip, those negative
tapes that played incessantly in your head are now breaking
down. You can hear more of the positives. At first, you may
be amazed at how much you have been missing. You may
be genuinely surprised to realize that you have gifts that are
genuinely valued by those around you. You may be even more
surprised when you feel yourself valuing your own talents.
Life, you will find, becomes so much more enjoyable when
you allow yourself to hear the good news.

When you rise above your sense of inadequacy, many beautiful changes take place. You will have made some important
alterations in yourself, but your biggest change is that you will
have come to accept yourself as you really are. Carl Rogers
called this the paradox of change: When you accept yourself
as you are, you change. Working through shame means becoming the real you. As we have seen, there are many rewards
for successfully sailing these waters. But there is at least one
other reward that I have not detailed, a very special gift given
to those who have struggled to accept themselves.

So many times I have seen people struggle to conquer
shame and, as the process unfolds, develop a mighty passion.
They move from spectator to player, observer to participant.
While previously far too self-conscious to risk a display of
emotion and commitment, once people conquer shame, there
is often an explosion of focused energy. Passion is the force
you feel when you begin to emerge as the person you are
meant to be. Passion erupts when your head, your heart, and
your conscience all point in the same direction. There may be
fear, but fear can seldom contain passion. Passion is triumph
over fear, but more than anything, passion is the conquest of
shame. Passion is the thunderous cry that says, "I will be what
I am to be! I will do what I am to do!" Your life force that was

cramped into such a small, dark space for so long will push you as if to make up for lost time.

Follow your passion. Follow it even when it takes you before those who might judge you. Follow your passion even if it takes you to places where you could fail. Follow it even if you are not completely sure where it is taking you. Your passion will lead you to the path with heart. It will lead you to places where you will make your most important contributions.

In all my work with people and their shame, it is this passion that has intrigued me most. In some it is a quiet passion that develops, while in others it is more like a lion's roar. Each time I see this force emerge, though, I am reminded how much shame takes from a person's life. Those who heal seem to have a natural inclination to make up for lost time. It also makes me wince as I think about all those who may never take the risks needed to heal.

The cost of living a life shrouded in shame is grotesque. The rewards for working through shame are magnificent.

Some Hardships Will Remain

Accepting yourself as good enough will not take all the pain out of life. Adversity will remain. Life will continue to challenge you. Understand this. As you come to respect yourself, your life will improve dramatically but there will still be struggles. You will continue to age and be subject to the ailments that aging brings. You will have to deal with physical limitations and unpleasant life experiences. It's doubtful that all your decisions will be the right ones, and you will have to live with the consequences of your mistakes. There will be suffering around you. You will know the frustrations and sadness of living in an imperfect world. There will be loss in your life. You have allowed yourself to connect with people, and these attachments will add a great deal to your life. Still, where there is closeness, there is the potential for loss. With each loss, you will redecide if it is worth getting close to people. You do know, however, what it is like to isolate yourself. Hopefully, you will choose to stay close to people.

No matter how much self-confidence you build, you will not be able to erase painful memories. Those memories will have less power and control over you, but they will still be there. You may continue to be sensitive or introverted, but even if you would not have chosen these personality traits, it is now easier to live with them. Sensitive people are more easily hurt, true. But they have wonderful abilities to understand the needs of others. You can now see the good that comes with being sensitive. And there is nothing wrong with being introverted. You may never be outgoing enough to run for president, but introverts can be very creative and they make for very loyal friends. Maybe you would like to be a little more thick-skinned or more of a social butterfly. But instead you realize that the real you is quite different. Sometimes, you find that the real you is not what you had hoped it would be. This can be frustrating and disappointing. Please keep in mind, always, that the real you (even if it contains qualities you may not have asked for) is the person you are meant to be.

You must accept what you cannot change. This gets easier as you free yourself from the belief that everything about you is unacceptable. A blemish is just a blemish; it doesn't mean you are completely scarred.

I would like to tell you that life gets safer after shame leaves, but this isn't the case either. When you felt inadequate, you were safe and miserable. If your self-loathing was severe enough, you may have put yourself in danger, but you really didn't think you were risking much. You don't fear losing something that has no value. But with shame behind you, you accept more challenges. It's not that you like failure, but you are willing to risk it in order to learn what you need to learn, accomplish what you need to accomplish, get to know those whom you need to get to know. You feel fear but it doesn't stop you as it once did. You risk more now. You value more of yourself. But even when you risk and fail, you still value the person you are. When you feel you are good enough, you enter the jungle of life. You walk with your head up, confident (but not overly confident) in your ability to survive. You are capable of giving and receiving affirmation. You can be gentle with yourself while making demands on yourself. You can accomplish and then feel good about your accomplishments. You face fear because you know that human beings grow by challenging fear. There was a time in your life when making an honest inventory of your flaws was overwhelming. Now, while still frightening, you are no longer defeated before the process begins. You can look at yourself to learn which areas have room for growth and which dimensions may call for an acceptance of imperfection. Ernest Kurtz and Katherine Ketcham describe this well in their book *The Spirituality of Imperfection:* "To be human is to be imperfect, yet yearn for completion; it is to be uncertain, yet long for certainty; to be imperfect yet long for perfection; to be broken yet crave wholeness."[15] You accept that you may never be perfect but this doesn't stop you from growing. You no longer need an unattainable perfection in order to feel adequate. You can be human, flawed, wounded, and more than good enough.

The Most Important Lessons You've Learned in Life

It is important that as you move ahead, you do not forget what you have lived. There are vital lessons to be learned from

your life. Often people make the mistake of trying to leave
Shame City like the proverbial bat out of hell. While this is
understandable, it is also unfortunate. Recovery from shame
does not mean developing amnesia. It does not involve brain
surgery that destroys your memory. Rather, healing means taking a turn in your path while maintaining an awareness of the
road that has led you to the present. Never insist that you
forget the life you have lived. If you do, you will be disappointed in yourself because your mind will want to hold on
to all your experiences. It does so in an ongoing attempt to
learn from life.

It has been said that the essence of mental health is the
ability to learn from experience. When we learn from experience, our lives become a growing process where mistakes are
less likely to be repeated and the most important lessons are
recognized and valued. Growth requires a willingness to learn.
Learning provides the knowledge needed to become who we
are meant to be.

Growth involves learning from life. It means being aware
of the lessons of life as they pass before us. Then comes the
second crucial step: living those lessons. This means apply-
ing and practicing the knowledge you have acquired. Lifelong
growth requires knowledge and effort. Take what life teaches
you. Learn it. Live it. Over the past five years or so, I have
given a number of workshops that focus on the question:
"What is the Most Important Lesson You Have Learned in
Life?" Some people know the answer immediately. Others
have to think a while. The point of the exercise, though,
is to make people aware of what life has taught them. It also
forces people to consider whether or not they live what they
have learned.

Over the years I have heard hundreds, perhaps thousands, of these lessons. I am grateful to all those who have

shared their wisdom. The following are some examples of this wisdom.

- Never give up.

- Listen to the voice of God.

- Love.

- Learn to forgive.

- Fear can be conquered.

- Others are not responsible for my happiness.

- Don't be a victim of circumstances. Take charge of your life.

- Be true to yourself.

- Truth gives wings to the soul.

- Have respect and reverence for life.

- Live gratitude.

Often these lessons are expressed with strength and passion as if they carry an energy of their own. And once you look at the most important lessons you have learned in life, other valuable lessons usually come to mind. I then suggest that one of the healthiest things we can do for ourselves is identify the ten most important lessons we have learned in life. I advise them to build the list carefully. Keep it near them. Look at it often. This list tells us about ourselves. And to this day, I have never seen two identical lists. I guess everyone's path really is unique.

If you ever write a list of your own, you must ask yourself: "Am I living what I have learned?"

As the years go by, your list may change. Let it. Growth

means change. Each change presents you with a new experience and at least one new lesson. With every lesson you learn,
you become a little healthier.

Just the other day a man who had spent many years feeling
bad about himself told me that the most important lesson he
had learned in his life was that "God loves me." He said this
with conviction in his voice and a tear in his eye. Then, after
a moment or two of silence he added, "There are still some
times when I forget this, but I really know it is true."

This is a common occurrence. Hard times can produce
essential lessons. Lessons learned must then become lessons
lived. As we live these lessons, they become a part of who
we are. We may lose these lessons at times, but if we have
lived them, they are less likely to be gone forever. One of the
biggest mistakes you can make in your recovery from shame
is to give in to the temptation to forget everything about
this difficult time in your life. To maximize your health and
happiness, you must learn from all the facets of your life, even
the worst of times. Shame is an awful experience, but it can
teach you many things. While we all find our own gold in this
dark mine, there are a few valuable nuggets that seem to be
available to all who have survived inadequacy.

You have probably learned by now how much your thoughts
influence your feelings. When you are convinced you are
unlovable, your emotions all seem to turn painful. But you
now understand that you can direct your thoughts. You can
decide to stop your negative thinking by attacking it whenever it surfaces. You can choose to think positively. You can
choose to hope, look for the best in people (including yourself), and dig to find happy memories. There may have been a
time in your life when it seemed that someone else controlled
your thinking, a time when someone else's disapproval of you
became your own disapproval of yourself. Now you know that

you can take control of your thinking. If someone is going to control your thinking, it might as well be you.

Becoming good enough does not mean removing all your flaws. In fact, as you come to feel good enough, you may become aware of faults you never realized you had. But as shame leaves, these flaws no longer define you. Being good enough means developing a new perspective on your limitations. You can accept that some of your shortcomings may be permanent. This doesn't make you inadequate. It just means you are human. Being good enough means developing the humility to accept your humanness. On the other hand, you now know that some of your flaws can be corrected and you are capable of correcting them. You are now willing to invest the work needed to improve yourself. Getting better is always possible. You can get better, and better, and better.

Rising above shame means having faith in your goodness and faith in your ability to keep growing. When you can honestly say to yourself, "I am a good person and I can grow," you will know you have truly become good enough.

Final Thoughts

Once you begin to heal and after the initial fear dissolves, you may feel a burst of energy. You are a beautiful eagle now freed from a cage. The door opens and the real you bursts to the surface. This is your spiritual birthday, the time in your life when you begin to run toward becoming the person you are meant to be. As this process unfolds energy builds, energy that leads to empowerment. In spite of this energy you will still make mistakes, get sick, become confused at times, and occasionally feel shamed. Some people even report that in the earliest stages of recovery, things get worse before they get better. At this point you might feel vulnerable, exposed, and as some say, "just different." But as your healing continues, you feel freer, lighter, and more certain that you are headed in the right direction. As your personal power builds, you will deal effectively with the flaws in your life and the obstacles on your path. When you feel good about yourself, life doesn't really get easier; you just get better at dealing with it. The burst of energy that emerges early in recovery will eventually settle. You move into a new phase of your life and the newfound freedom that creates such exuberance grows into a stable lifestyle. The honeymoon gives way to a new life. Your life.

There will be a pull to forget your painful past. This would be a mistake. Denying your past would mean avoiding a significant part of yourself. No more secrets. No more hiding. Maintain an awareness of your past. Look at it through the eyes of a strong survivor. If you deal with them, the hard times can actually strengthen you. Never forget what you have been through. The difficult times can keep you humble, grounded, and sensitive to others. Knowing what it is like to be wounded can also make you a good friend to yourself and to others. When you grow through inferiority, you emerge as the person you are meant to be. The hanging judge in your head, who evaluated all your moves, has retired. The days of second-guessing every single decision are over. Instead of spending all your waking hours looking for evidence of your defectiveness, you now welcome affirmation and information that continues to confirm your worth as a good human being. You are no longer forcing everyone into the role of your critic. When you grow through inadequacy, you find that your life can be wonderful. You become grateful for the life you once ridiculed.

If this sounds too good to be true, then you may still be early in your recovery. You have no doubt noticed that this book is just about finished, and yet you are aware that there may be quite a bit of work left to do. But you see, I have written another book for you that will continue to work with you as your healing continues. You are holding that book in your hands right now. Each time you read this book it will be different. It is meant to stay with you as you work toward believing in yourself. You may still be saying, "I'm not sure it's possible." After reading this a second time, you may say, "Perhaps I can." By a third or fourth reading, hopefully, you will be well into recovery. Reading alone, of course, will not take you where you need to be. Healing is about understanding, deciding, and doing. Above all, always look for good people to help you.

If you choose to read this again, please do so with a critical eye. We have all traveled through shame in our own unique ways. You may have experiences and conclusions that I have not covered. Make sure, however, that you include these in your story. A man in the process of recovering from shame once told me, "I used to think that the only thing that loved me was food." You may identify immediately with this remark. Or the thought may be completely foreign to you. Those of us who have done shame have all done it a little differently. Think of this book as a grocery store. Look around but take only what you need. Later, you may come back for some more items. As you develop more and more faith in yourself, you will become increasingly effective in selecting what you need to live a happier, healthier life. You have the energy you need to become the person you are meant to be. You have the power to be more than good enough. A biologist I once knew put it this way: "At the moment you were conceived, of all the thousands of sperm cells that were fighting for the job, you were the fastest and the strongest." If you didn't have what it takes to be adequate, you wouldn't be here. You may never be perfect, but there is no need to apologize for your existence. You have everything you need to become everything you need to be. Believe it.

Don't try to change too much of yourself. Look for good people to be a part of your life. Have faith in your ability to keep growing. Have faith in your goodness.

Notes

1. H. M. Lynd, *On Shame and the Search for Identity* (New York: Harcourt, Brace & Co., 1958), 25.

2. A. P. Morrison, *The Culture of Shame* (New York: Ballantine Books, 1996), 13.

3. D. L. Nathanson, ed., *The Many Faces of Shame* (New York: Guilford Press, 1987).

4. G. Kaufman, *The Psychology of Shame* (New York: Springer Publishing Co., 1989).

5. M. Lewis, *Shame: The Exposed Self* (New York: Free Press, 1995), 34.

6. H. L. Ansbacher and R. R. Ansbacher, eds., *The Individual Psychology of Alfred Adler* (New York: Harper & Row, Publishers, 1956), 257.

7. Ibid., 258.

8. Kaufman, *The Psychology of Shame,* 44.

9. E. S. Schneidman, *The Suicidal Mind* (New York: Oxford University Press, 1996), 133.

10. D. L. Nathanson, "Shaming Systems in Couples, Families, and Institutions," in *The Many Faces of Shame,* ed. Nathanson, 266.

11. Lynd, *On Shame and the Search for Identity,* 66.

12. Morrison, *The Culture of Shame,* 108.

13. B. Flanigan, *Forgiving the Unforgivable* (New York: Macmillan, 1992), 121.

14. Ibid., 125.

15. E. Kurtz and K. Ketcham, *The Spirituality of Imperfection* (New York: Bantam Books, 1994).